Building Trust, Maki

Four Group Activity Manuals for High Risk Students

Della the Dinosaur Talks About Violence and Anger Management

(Grades K-6)

Johnson Institute
7205 Ohms Lane
Minneapolis, MN 55439-2159

Library of Congress Cataloging-in-Publication Data

Schmidt, Teresa M.
Della the Dinosaur talks about violence and anger management (grades K-6) / Teresa M. Schmidt and Thelma W. Spencer.
p. cm.—(Building trust, making friends)
Includes bibliographical references.
ISBN 1-56246-021-8
1. Family violence—Study and teaching (Elementary)—United States. 2. Family violence—Prevention—Study and teaching (Elementary)—United States. 3. Anger—Study and teaching (Elementary)—United States. 4. Social group work—United States. I. Spencer, Thelma W. II. Title. III. Series: Schmidt, Teresa M. Building trust, making friends.
HQ809.3.U5S36 1991
362.82'92-dc20 91-36750
CIP

PRINTED IN THE UNITED STATES OF AMERICA

98 97 96 / 6 5 4 3

Building Trust, Making Friends

Four Group Activity Manuals
for High Risk Students

Della the Dinosaur Talks About Violence and Anger Management

(Grades K-6)

by

Teresa M. Schmidt and Thelma W. Spencer

JOHNSON INSTITUTE®

Minneapolis

Contents

Acknowledgments

The authors would like to thank Superintendent Donald S. Bruno and the Pupil Services Department of Newport News Public Schools, Newport News, Virginia, for their support and commitment to establishing a group counseling program.

We are also grateful for the willingness of the IMPACT Staff of Newport News Public Schools to participate in the original field testing of this material. Additionally, we offer thanks to the many children who participated in that field testing. Their enthusiasm and ideas enriched the materials.

Gratitude is also expressed to the guidance counselors in York County Public Schools, York County, Virginia, whose suggestions, comments, and questions enriched the work.

Recognition goes to Jayne H. Easley, M.Ed., who holds degrees in child development, counseling, and psychology, and who assisted in the development of the Della the Dinosaur stories. Mrs. Easly has served as a board member for Alternatives, Inc., a drug intervention agency, and presently serves as Parent Educator Coordinator for the York Cooperative Preschool.

Likewise, recognition also goes to Carolyn Krol, R.N., M.S.W., L.C.S.W., who provided consultation during the development of this curriculum. Ms. Krol is the director of Oyster Point Counseling Center, a training supervisor for the Family Therapy Practice Center of Washington, D.C., and a clinical supervisor for the American Association of Marriage and Family Therapists. She has served on the board of the Virginia Peninsula Council for Domestic Violence and leads a support group for the staff members of the Battered Women's Shelter, Hampton, Virginia. She has presented workshops about family violence on the local and state level. Ms. Krol generously shared her ideas and expertise.

Finally, we offer thanks to Matthew and Thomas Schmidt and Leigh Spencer for their consultation, advice, great patience and faith, and expertise on dinosaurs.

About the Authors

Teresa M. Schmidt, M.S.W., L.C.S.W., B.C.D., has been a clinical social worker since 1970. A graduate of the College of William and Mary and the Smith College School for Social Work, Ms. Schmidt has had extensive experience in out-patient settings. Bringing her clinical experience in mental health to Newport News Public Schools, Newport News, Virginia, in 1987, she worked with Dr. Thelma Spencer to develop and implement in a school setting a prevention/intervention group program for children from chemically dependent families. Ms. Schmidt is coauthor with Dr. Spencer of the *Building Trust, Making Friends* series: *Peter the Puppy Talks About Chemical Dependence in the Family, Tanya Talks About Chemical Dependence in the Family, Thomas Barker Talks About Divorce and Separation,* and *Della the Dinosaur Talks About Violence and Anger Management.* Ms. Schmidt currently lives in the cornfields of Indiana, where she maintains a private practice, consults to local school systems on leading support groups, and conducts training workshops for mental health and school professionals on the local, state, and national level. Her most recent books are *Anger Management and Violence Prevention* and *Changing Families,* group activities manuals for middle and high school students published by the Johnson Institute in 1993 and 1994.

Thelma W. Spencer, Ed.D., C.S.A.C., has been an educator and counselor for over twenty years, working with special populations in a variety of settings. She gained clinical experience in substance abuse counseling while earning her doctorate from the College of William and Mary. Dr. Spencer oversees the Substance Abuse Prevention/Intervention Program for Newport News Public Schools. She is on the adjunct faculty of the University of Virginia and is a consultant for the Southeast Regional Center for Drug-Free Schools and the Virginia Department of Education Alcohol and Other Drug Abuse Prevention Project. Dr. Spencer was honored as the 1990 Outstanding Student Assistance Professional by the National Organization of Student Assistance Programs and Professionals.

The *Building Trust, Making Friends* group model was developed by Ms. Schmidt and Dr. Spencer and was field tested in the Newport News Public Schools, Newport News, Virginia. Through a unique, structured format and progression of themes, the model makes use of clinical and educational theory as well as practical experience to provide intervention and prevention services to at-risk children.

Introduction

Children are at risk. Too many of them. Growing up in homes tinged by the sad effects of chemical dependence,[1] parental separation and divorce, and family violence, these children will face many problems. As a teacher, school social worker, psychologist, guidance counselor, Core Team member, or member of a Student Assistance Program (SAP), it is only natural for you to feel concerned for these children. It is only right that you seek new ways to help them.

You have many wishes for these children. You wish that you could walk with them, be a support to them, be a friend to them, help them in their decision making, keep them safe. You wish that everyone would recognize and see them as special, talented, wonder-filled, precious. Thankfully, many people share your concerns and wishes for at-risk children. More than that, like you, many people are working hard to help turn your concern into confidence and make your wishes come true.

With concerns and wishes like yours in mind, *Building Trust, Making Friends* has been developed for at-risk children from chemically dependent families, from separated or divorced families, and from families in which violence is used to express anger. *Building Trust, Making Friends* consists of four group-model programs. Three of the programs are aimed at children in grades K-6; the fourth is for children in grades 6-8. Each program is based on an eleven-session group model that uses both clinical and educational theory to help at-risk children.

At-risk children share similar beliefs and perspectives. In an effort to create order out of the chaos that is too often so common in at-risk families, the children tend to blame

[1] The term *chemical dependence,* as used in this manual, refers to any and all dependence on any and all mind-altering substances, in particular, alcohol and other drugs. Major medical, psychiatric, public health, hospital, and psychological associations have pronounced dependence on alcohol—or alcoholism—a *disease.* The American Medical Society on Alcoholism and Other Drug Dependencies (1987) has officially declared that what is true for alcoholism is true for addiction to other drugs. Chemical dependence has certain describable characteristics. Namely, it is a disease that is: (1) compulsive-obsessive; (2) primary; (3) progressive; (4) chronic; (5) fatal; and (6) treatable. The following may be considered a working definition of the disease of chemical dependence: if the use of alcohol and other drugs is interfering with any area of a person's life—whether social (legal, school, work, family, or friends) or personal (physical, mental, emotional, or spiritual)—and he or she can't stop using without help, then the person is chemically dependent.

themselves for the problem, whether it's chemical dependence, divorce, or violence. Children also tend to believe that they can control, change, or cure the family's problem. The group model corrects these common misconceptions. Children seem better able to understand new information—information that allows them to change their beliefs—when it is presented in small groups.

The group model also helps children learn how to become aware of their feelings, how to express them appropriately, how to grow in self-esteem, and how to acquire the interactive skills and value systems necessary to function as healthy human beings. The group model engages the children in both the cognitive and the affective sides of learning. It gives the children forums where they can discuss problems and receive age-appropriate information about their family's problem. The group model supplies a safe and supportive environment and empowers the children to grow and heal.

Each of the four programs in *Building Trust, Making Friends* features a format, structure, and progression of themes designed to meet the needs of at-risk children:

1. *Peter the Puppy Talks About Chemical Dependence in the Family* meets the needs of children (grades K-6) from chemically dependent families.
2. *Tanya Talks About Chemical Dependence in the Family* is designed for middle school children (grades 6-8) from chemically dependent families.
3. *Thomas Barker Talks About Divorce and Separation* helps children (grades K-6) from divorced, separated, single-parent, or stepfamilies.
4. *Della the Dinosaur Talks About Violence and Anger Management* is helpful both for children (grades K-6) whose families use violence to express anger and for children who themselves exhibit aggressive behavior.

This complete and easy-to-use manual contains all you need to lead a group of at-risk kindergarten through sixth-graders through the program *Della the Dinosaur Talks About Violence and Anger Management.*

Part One of this manual contains materials to help you understand the dynamics of the group model, including group format and progression of session themes. It also provides guidelines and materials to help you implement the program in your school or agency.

Part Two contains materials both to help you understand the issues affecting children from violent families and to help you identify children from violent families. It also contains the complete group guide for leading a Della the Dinosaur Group. The group guide includes the objectives, necessary preparations, background information and guidelines, and detailed step-by-step session plans for each of the eleven sessions.

Part Three contains support materials, a list of references and supplementary readings, and a list of important resources. This section will further help group leaders and other staff make the group process successful and rewarding for everyone involved.

Overall, this manual provides sound, practical, creative, and innovative ways to help children correct their misconceptions, meet their emotional needs, deal effectively with their problems, and grow to live lives that are much less "at risk."

PART ONE

Establishing a Support Group Program for At-Risk Children

Chapter 1: Dynamics of the *Building Trust, Making Friends* Group Model

Perhaps the most effective and practical setting for this group model is in the school. This is the case for a variety of reasons. First, many families undergoing the stress of chemical dependence or violence deny it and don't seek professional help. Second, even families who aren't in denial often lack the ability or means to make use of professional help. Third, many professional helping facilities, such as treatment centers for chemical dependence, aren't equipped to work with children. Fourth, the organizational structure of many professional helping facilities often doesn't allow people who do have the skills and training to deal with children access to them. Better than any other setting, schools are in a position to offer prevention services—like this program—to the large numbers of at-risk children who would otherwise never receive them.

Schools can offer the group model's services as part of a comprehensive prevention program implemented by pupil services personnel, which include clinical and school social workers, school psychologists, guidance counselors, and chemical dependence counselors. Student Assistance Programs (SAPs) and Core Teams will also find the program's group model ideal to use and easy to implement.

Although the school is a valuable setting for this group model, it may be used elsewhere: in chemical dependence treatment centers that provide family services, in mental health centers, in private practices, and in battered women's shelters.

The same group model is used in all four programs of *Building Trust, Making Friends.* It is a dynamic process that helps meet the needs of children from at-risk families by providing structure, consistency, predictability, and fun. It incorporates a structured format that remains the same for all group sessions. The group model also presents a specific and definite progression of themes that fosters nonjudgmental education about the particular issue at hand, corrects misconceptions that children commonly have regarding the issue, and teaches children effective coping strategies that enable them to let go of futile "overresponsibility" and begin to take care of themselves.

All this takes place through the medium of stories told by either a make-believe animal or a fictional human student. The children can easily identify with these "characters" without feeling disloyal to their own families. The group model enables children who come from families in which they're feeling the severe stress of chemical dependence, parental separation and divorce, or violence to recognize that they're not alone, that other children have feelings just like theirs, and that, above all, they can learn to manage their feelings and deal with them in healthy ways.

Group Format

The group model presented in this manual follows a structured format for each group session that is both educationally and clinically sound. The three-part format includes the same components.

1. Beginning the Session
    - Group rules (reviewed each session)
    - Centering exercise
    - Feelings check-in
    - Review of basic facts (beginning with Session 2)
2. Exploring the Story
    - Story (the heart of the session)
    - Group discussion
    - Follow-up activity
    - Worksheet for reinforcing basic facts
3. Wrapping Up
    - Repetition of centering exercise
    - Affirmation
    - Closing activity

Since the format and its components remain virtually constant through all the sessions, these components deserve a closer look.

Group Rules and Rules Contract. Creating an atmosphere in which a group of children (some of whom might not know each other) feel secure and willing to share thoughts and feelings is a major undertaking. Many children will have never participated in a group process before, so they'll be unaccustomed to the expectations and the boundaries of a group.

Group rules ensure that all group members will be treated with the dignity and respect they deserve. Group rules also establish a standard of behavior for group members. They establish the expectation that children can be responsible for their behavior and participation in the group.

The group leader presents the rules in contract form and asks the children to agree to them by signing their names to the contract. Rules are displayed in the group meeting room. At the beginning of each group session, the leader reviews them, making sure that the children understand them all. The consistency of this practice reminds the children that they're safe in group, that the rules serve to protect them, and that all group members will behave as they've agreed to behave by signing the contract.

Centering Exercise. This exercise sets the stage for group work in a positive way. The techniques learned in the centering exercise, which include deep breathing and tensing and relaxing muscles, are not limited to group work only. Once mastered, children can use them in "real-life" situations. Repeated toward the end of a group session, the centering exercise not only reinforces learning but also enables the children to calm down—especially if intense feelings arose during the session—and helps them get ready to return to their regular classroom.

Feelings Check-in. During the feelings check-in the children learn to identify, own, and express feelings in appropriate ways. The group leader validates, accepts, and tolerates the children's feelings. For example, responding to a child who says he wants to hit his mother because she yelled at him, the group leader might say, 'It sounds like you're feeling very angry. Can you tell us what you're angry about?" After the child responds, the group leader could continue, "Many children feel angry when that happens to them. But it's important to choose a helpful way to express your anger or to use it to work for you. We'll learn more about anger in Sessions 6 and 7." Again, if a child is tearful because a grandparent has died, the group leader can say, "Many children feel sad or lonely when a grandparent dies. They might show their sadness by crying or by drawing a picture or writing a poem. After a while, they don't feel as sad. We'll learn more about feelings in Session 5."

By accepting and validating feelings and by helping the children identify helpful ways to express feelings, the group leader consistently teaches that feelings aren't bad or dangerous, that they can be felt and expressed, and that they will pass. Thus, the feelings check-in functions both as a corrective and a therapeutic experience for the children.

Review of Basic Facts. Beginning with Session 2, the basic facts learned in previous sessions are reviewed for understanding. This regular repetition and clarification is an effective technique to help even very young children learn and use the key concepts presented in the sessions.

Story (Bibliotherapy). Bibliotherapy simply means "healing story." The story or bibliotherapy uses an appealing make-believe animal (for elementary-aged groups) or a fictional student (for middle school groups) to present basic facts about chemical dependence, divorce and separation, sexual abuse, or violence and the effects of these situations on the family. Most of the children will be able to identify easily with the characters without feeling that they're betraying their family. Even tough, streetwise children experience fun, warmth, and affection with the characters.

Discussion. Each session's story is followed by questions the leader may use to initiate group discussion. In the discussion, the children have the chance to process the story, and the group leader has the chance to make sure they understand the concepts and issues presented.

Activity. Using the Activity Sheets provided, the activity reinforces the material presented in the story. In a nonthreatening way, it encourages the children to express their perceptions of their situation, but only to the degree they can and want to share them.

Basic Facts Worksheet. The Basic Facts Worksheet is a verbal, visual, and auditory tool that reinforces the basic facts the story has presented and the children have discussed. A new worksheet with new basic facts is presented each week and the basic facts are then repeated and explained in following weeks during the Review of Basic Facts. The worksheet also serves to build the children's positive self-esteem. Unlike worksheets the children might receive in a regular class in school (for example, an arithmetic worksheet), these worksheets are "fail-safe," designed to enable the children to get the "right" answer every time.

Affirmation. This gives the children a chance to end the group session on a positive note, even if intense feelings arose during the session. The affirmation reinforces the content presented in the session and helps the children learn to choose a positive attitude.

Closing. The closing exercise helps the group develop a sense of bonding, cohesiveness, acceptance, and sharing. It allows for physical touch in a safe, nonthreatening atmosphere, which may be a new experience for many of the children. The same closing exercise concludes each session.

This structured format encourages the children to participate as fully as possible in the group process. Go-arounds, where everybody has a chance to describe art work, writing, feelings, and so on, are used extensively to make it easy for group members to share in a safe, nonthreatening way. Although the children are never forced to take part and are given the right to "pass," the format allows each group member at least three opportunities per session to speak and other, non-verbal, opportunities to participate as well. The repeated structure of all group sessions provides a sense of predictability and consistency that is often absent in the homes of at-risk children.

Progression of Themes

The essence of the program's group model is the progression of themes. In Sessions 1 and 2, the program presents the children with education and information about the issues of chemical dependence, separation or divorce, or violence. In Session 3, the program describes how the stresses of chemical dependence, separation or divorce, or violence affect children and their families. Session 4 addresses and corrects misconceptions common among such at-risk children. Then, in Sessions 5-7, the program shifts its focus to identifying, validating, and accepting the children's feelings about their situations. Two of these sessions (6 and 7) help children see anger as a positive force. In Sessions 8-11, the program turns to teaching the children coping strategies, showing them how to detach from futile and overwhelming feelings of responsibility and empowering them, in age-appropriate and positive ways, to take care of themselves.

The themes combine to create a program that helps the children become less at risk, while never making them feel that they're being disloyal to their families. In fact, the group leader never asks the children to reveal negative things about their family, nor does the leader ever make negative comments about people who use alcohol or other drugs, who are separated or divorced, or who use violence. The program consistently describes family members' behaviors objectively and nonjudgmentally. At the same time, the program unfailingly identifies and validates the feelings in children—and other family members—that such behaviors elicit.

Each group program follows the same, specific thematic progression:

Sessions 1-2: Presenting basic facts and information about a specific issue (chemical dependence, divorce, violence in the home)

Session 3: Describing and assessing the impact or effects of the specific issue on the family and the child

Session 4: Correcting common misconceptions

Session 5: Dealing with the feelings the children experience

Sessions 6-7: Managing anger

Session 8: Coping strategies

Session 9: Setting personal goals

Session 10: Group Presentation—Optional

Session 11: Developing a support system

In Sessions 1-2, the make-believe animal or the fictional student presents the children with information on a particular issue such as chemical dependence, divorce, or anger. The character also helps the children identify positive ways of feeling better.

In Session 3, the make-believe animal or the fictional student describes his or her own family, the stress or trauma a particular issue has caused in the family, and the ways other family members have behaved in reaction to the stress or trauma.

In Session 4, the make-believe animal or the fictional student and the children meet a helping professional (Mrs. Owl), who helps to correct the misconceptions common in families affected by the particular issue. Together with the make-believe animal or the fictional student, the children discover that although they can't cure the family's problems, they can do some things to help themselves.

Sessions 5-7 focus on feelings and emotions. Session 5 concentrates on helping the children identify, validate, and come to accept and tolerate their feelings. Sessions 6-7 deal with ways to manage anger by helping the children discover how to express anger in personally helpful ways. They learn to see anger as an energy or power that they can use to work for them, and they learn how to express anger in helpful ways so they can let it go.

Session 8 deals with coping strategies and gives specific examples of situations that at-risk families experience. The children learn about age-appropriate ways to be responsible for themselves and, in particular, how to ask for help when they need it. They also learn how to keep themselves safe, how to avoid assuming responsibility for someone else's feelings or behavior, and how to do good things for themselves.

The objective of Session 9 is to help the children learn how to set personal goals. Children identify ways they can take good care of their bodies, minds, feelings, and choices.

Session 10 is an *optional* session that gives the children an opportunity to offer their own presentation of the many facts and skills they have learned throughout the group process. When children teach someone else the basic facts they have learned, their own learning increases as does their self-esteem. The children's presentation also helps to raise the level of the audience's learning and awareness, and it encourages future referrals. Audiences can range from a single person—a principal or administrator—to a class of students, to an entire grade level. The presentation is very appropriate for prevention purposes. The group members present only facts. They do not reveal anything personal about either themselves or their families.

In Session 11, the children celebrate their learning and growth. They create their own support system, a "yellow pages," that will help them know where to go and to whom to turn for help when they need it in the future.

Displacement Communication

In its progression of themes, the group model uses a therapeutic technique called *displacement communication* (Kalter 1990)[2] to help children deal with family stress, while allowing them to remain loyal to their families. Lacking knowledge and perspective, children are not often verbal or articulate in describing family problems or their reactions to those problems. Even if children possessed such knowledge and perspective, they still might not want to discuss the problems, both in an effort to avoid or deny their own distress and in an effort to preserve their family's good name. Children are often unaware of their specific feelings and are unable to name them. They're also unaware of their internal conflicts, and end up acting them out by fighting, misbehaving, somatizing, overeating, or trying to be perfect.

Recognizing that children don't communicate directly, the group model also uses an indirect method of communicating with them, by means of a "displacement figure"—either a stuffed animal or a fictional teenager—who tells its story in the group sessions.

Displacement communication contains the following six steps:

1. Represent in the displacement figure (toy, doll, fictional child) the behaviors that signify emotional distress (fighting, crying, temper tantrums).
2. Acknowledge how upsetting such behavior is to the displacement figure.
3. Address the displacement figure's underlying conflict or emotional pain.
4. Correct any misperceptions in the displacement.
5. Accept conflicted feelings.
6. Present alternative ways of expressing and coping with conflict.

These steps are incorporated in the group model's sessions.

In the sessions, in a nonjudgmental way, the displacement characters (make-believe animal or fictional student) are educated about a particular issue (chemical dependence, divorce, or family violence). The characters describe their family stress and their behavior and acknowledge how painful that behavior is. Mrs. Owl, the helping professional, identifies the underlying conflict and the emotional pain common to children in the characters' situation. She then corrects their misconceptions and misperceptions by teaching them the three Cs: children don't cause and can't control or change parental chemical dependence or divorce or violence. Mrs. Owl goes on to teach the characters how to identify, accept, and express their feelings in appropriate ways. Finally, she teaches alternative coping strategies to enable the characters to deal more successfully with their stress.

---

[2]Where pertinent, throughout this manual, the contribution of experts is acknowledged by citing the *person's last name* and the *date of the specific source material.* References for these citations may be found by checking the name and date, listed alphabetically, in the References and Suggested Readings section of this manual on pages 231-232.

The children easily identify with the appealing characters. Without having to admit it, the children can compare themselves to the character's behavior and situation. Due to the program's nonthreatening and nonjudgmental nature, the children are able to use new ideas without feeling pressured. They are able to save face and to get help without feeling disloyal to their family.

Benefits of Use

Using the *Building Trust, Making Friends* group model for at-risk children can benefit your school on a number of levels, including the logistics level, the individual level, and the system level.

The Logistics Level. Logistically, the model provides structure for new and untrained group leaders. The materials contained in the manual provide everything a leader will need to implement a group, including a self-referral group survey form for classroom surveys, a parental consent letter, a screening interview outline, and complete guidelines for each session.

The structure of the group format cuts down considerably on behavior problems during group session. Generally, children (from kindergarten through eighth grade) enjoy participating in these groups and eagerly recommend them to their friends.

The Individual Level. Children who participate in the program have benefited in a variety of ways, including the following: (1) children's behavior in school improved, as evidenced by fewer trips to the office and fewer suspensions; (2) children increased their attachment to school, which has proved to be effective drop-out prevention; (3) middle school students were helped to abstain from alcohol, marijuana, and other drugs; and (4) children integrated concepts taught in the group into other situations. The examples that follow illustrate how children were able to integrate concepts taught in the group into other situations.

Stephen, a fifth-grader, had been sent frequently to the principal's office due to behavior problems, before taking part in a Thomas Barker group for children from divorced or separated families. When, in group, Stephen encountered the basic fact called the 3 Cs (children can't cause, control, or change a parental separation or divorce), he bridled. "That's not true," he said. "At least when I act bad in school, my parents come and talk to each other." By the end of the group's session, however, Stephen had come a long way. "Well, I used to think a child could change a separation," Stephen said. "Now I know that's not true." Stephen was not seen in the principal's office during the entire time the Thomas Barker group met.

Donald, a kindergartner, was placed in a Della the Dinosaur group for children from homes where violence is used to express anger after being referred for his aggressive behavior in school. After hearing how Della sometimes stayed home from school to make sure no one got hurt, Donald said, "Sometimes when my parents fight, they don't send me to school. From now on, I'm going to call my aunt and have her take me to school." This example demonstrates how even the youngest children are able to grasp and integrate the concepts the program presents.

Angela, a first-grader, was referred to a Della the Dinosaur group after Angela's mother reported being physically abused by Angela's father. During group, when Angela learned the basic fact that parents usually love their children even when they are using violent ways to express their anger, she said, "That means when my dad shot through the window at my mom he still loves me."

A sixth-grade girl whose father murdered her eight-year-old brother taught her mother a relaxing technique learned in group ("Breathing Through Your Feet") to help her get through the trial.

After learning the basic fact that children should *wait* until a chemically dependent parent is sober before talking about how they feel, a sixth-grade boy in a Peter the Puppy group told his inebriated father one evening that he wouldn't talk to him until the next day (when the father would be sober).

Sometimes there is a ripple effect from a child's participation in one of the groups, and family members also benefit. One mother entered therapy because her son smiled when she asked him about his group experience. The child wouldn't discuss the group because of confidentiality, but the mother realized that he liked it and was benefiting from it.

The System Level. Since the group model recommends in-service programs for administrators and teachers about issues for children from at-risk families before beginning the groups in the school, the entire system can benefit from using the *Building Trust, Making Friends* group model.

In-servicing raises the awareness and education levels of teachers and administrators about the issues dealt with in the groups (chemical dependence, divorce, family violence). It also helps some who take part to identify for the first time that they are children from such families and to understand some of the problems that they've had or are still having in their own lives. Many who share in the in-service may have friends or relatives who are affected by someone else's chemical dependence, divorce, or violence. Thus, the in-service plants the seeds of recovery for many. Participants may be encouraged to gain further education about these particular issues (chemical dependence, divorce, family violence), to offer informed help to their students who come from chemically dependent, divorced, or violent families, and to seek any professional help they may need themselves.

Chapter 2: Implementing the Group Program

This chapter will help you implement the group program of *Building Trust, Making Friends* in your school, agency, or other counseling setting. The chapter includes information on acquiring administrative support, recruiting and training staff, developing a referral network, screening candidates, and forming and scheduling groups. You will also find information on informed consent, confidentiality, and self-disclosure on the part of group leaders. The chapter will also point out effective means of follow-up on the individual, group, and system level. Finally, it will outline ways you can use the program in guidance counseling and family therapy.

As mentioned earlier, although schools may be able to reach the largest numbers of children, the program may be used in a variety of other settings as well. After deciding where it will best fit in your school's (or agency's) situation, you must undertake the task of getting it started. The first step in doing that is gaining administrative support.

Gaining Administrative Support

You need administrative support. Without it, the program can't exist, let alone prosper. If building administrators aren't aware of the needs and characteristics of at-risk children, you can plan in-services to raise their awareness levels. Principals may feel that they're taking unnecessary risks by supporting groups for at-risk children, especially children from chemically dependent or violent families, and initially may not see any benefits for themselves. If you encounter this sort of resistance from principals, discuss with them the program's low-key profile but very real benefits and its long-term results.

If a school is to support the program, the principal's backing is necessary. If principals establish student support groups as a priority, they will direct teachers to allow children to leave the classroom in order to participate. Likewise, principals will also be prepared to answer questions from hostile, resistant, or concerned parents, although such calls are rare.

Offer an in-service to raise awareness levels. Describe how the program will benefit the children, their families, the school, and the community. Describe the common misconceptions that children from at-risk families often have. Explain how displacement communication is used to correct children's misconceptions, while allowing them to remain loyal to their families. Recount how youngsters who learn that they haven't caused, and can't be responsible for fixing, their family's problems will feel better about themselves, will perform better at school, and will be less likely to get into serious trouble either in school or in the community. Explain that learning coping strategies will help children take better care of themselves. Point out how school staffs are helped by their students' developing more positive attitudes about themselves and, thus, about learning. School staff members will feel good about referring students to groups that really work. Good groups will give both administrators and classroom teachers more free time to do their jobs.

If you're blessed with wholehearted administrative approval, it's still a good idea to provide in-service sessions for school personnel to acquaint them with the issues for at-risk children. Design a simple presentation describing the purposes of the program, the role of the group, and the dynamics of the group model, including the group format and progression of themes. The better school staff understand the program, the better will be their acceptance and support.

Staffing and Training

The authorization to provide prevention and intervention services for at-risk children can come from the superintendent or school board, in the form of drop-out prevention, substance abuse prevention, or services to at-risk children. The program will be enhanced if implemented by and with trained personnel. Effective staff may include members of Student Assistance Programs and Core Teams, social workers, psychologists, guidance counselors, chemical dependence counselors, nurses, Drug and Alcohol Resistance Education (DARE) officers, and teachers— all of whom can be trained to lead groups to help at-risk children. Although you'll have to depend on the staffing patterns of your school or agency, keep in mind that the needs of the children will be better met if personnel from various helping professions work together—not engage in territorial battles—to provide services.

The better trained your personnel, the better they'll be able to meet the needs of at-risk children. Training should include the following:

- information about the goals of the entire program
- education on specific issues to be dealt with in the groups (chemical dependence, divorce and separation, or family violence)
- instruction on how to lead groups
- ongoing supervision

One training model might require a three-hour graduate level course on substance abuse, twenty hours of in-service, and ten hours of supervised experience leading groups. Another model might consist of fifteen hours of experiential in-service, during which staff members lead and participate in the program's group sessions together. After this experience, they would be ready to co-lead a group with a certified worker. A third model might have a trainer provide staff development for new group leaders and in-services for school faculty at the beginning of the school year. The trainer then can assist new group leaders in developing referrals and screening potential group members. The trainer also leads a group, with a new leader observing. When the group is repeated during the second half of the school year, the new leader facilitates the group, with the trainer observing and providing supervision.

A fourth model meets the needs of professionals who are implementing this program by themselves. This model combines the expertise of different professionals as group co-leaders: for example, a teacher can co-lead a group with a chemical dependence counselor. The complementarity of skills, training, and experience will again better serve the needs of children.

Finally, you can also check your local resources for facilities that provide training. These may include chemical dependence treatment facilities, state and local health organizations, colleges and universities, and social welfare agencies. You can also find help by turning to a national organization, such as the Johnson Institute, which specializes in training. (See Resources for Help on page 235.)

Developing Referrals

Once you've gained administrative support and have begun training group leaders for the program, begin to develop a list of at-risk children who could benefit from being part of a group. You can build this list by looking to a number of referral sources, including the following:

- school-counseling/social-work case histories
- other school staff
- parents
- school children themselves
- broader community

School-Counseling/Social-Work Case Histories. Ask school counselors or social workers to recommend potential group members from their case loads.

Other School Staff. Look for referrals from any and all members of the school staff: building administrators, teachers, maintenance personnel, secretaries, DARE officers, Core Teams, school nurses. With the help of your in-services, all school staff members can learn to identify students who may be at-risk. By understanding how the group program operates and the services it provides, staff can refer children appropriately.

Parents. Some referrals will come directly from parents who might disclose during an interview or conference their stress over a family difficulty such as divorce, family violence, or chemical dependence. As leaders become more experienced in facilitating these groups, they gain confidence in asking about the presence of these problems in a family conference or history interview. Many parents will welcome the chance to have their children learn skills for healthy living. Introduce the groups as an educational and preventive service. To allay parents' fears that the groups might be intended to discover pathologies in their families, stress that the groups are clearly designed to educate and inform children, to correct their misconceptions, and to teach coping skills. Describe, too, the instructional process, including the use of the make-believe animal or the fictional student. This will help parents recognize that the group experience will be a positive one for their child, not a negative or judgmental one.

Schoolchildren Themselves. Another referral source is your school's student body. Self-referrals are likely to begin as soon as youngsters become aware of the program and its value. Offer classroom presentations on the various groups you plan to offer. Once the children understand what the groups are about, they'll find it easier to self-refer.

Simply arrange to visit a classroom. Begin your presentation by announcing to the children that you will be offering some groups during the school year, and that you want the children to know about them. To give the children a taste for what happens in group, lead them in a centering exercise (for example, "Breathing Through Your Feet," page 42). Then introduce one of the fictional characters, for example, Thomas Barker, by showing the children the stuffed toy animal. Describe some things Thomas likes to do with his family: play soccer with his dad; play puppy monopoly with his mom and sister. Then go on to describe what happens when his parents tell him they plan to separate: Thomas goes to school but doesn't feel like eating or playing at recess, and almost bursts into tears during science class. Show the children the stuffed toy animal, Mrs. Owl, and explain that she is a helping professional whom Thomas meets. Tell the children that Mrs. Owl teaches Thomas that he didn't cause his parents' separation and can't do anything to change or control it. Explain, too, that Mrs. Owl helps Thomas learn how to deal with his feelings in ways that will help him.

Depending on which groups you'll be offering, repeat the above process by introducing each of the other make-believe animals (Peter the Puppy and Della the Dinosaur) and the stresses in their lives. Be assured that children enjoy meeting the characters represented by the stuffed toy animals.

After your presentation, distribute copies of the Self-referral Group Survey Form (see page 228), and go through the directions on the form with the children. Ask all the children to sign the referral form, fold it in half, and return it to you, even if they are not interested in being in a group. The children who are interested in being in a group should check the group, or groups, they want to be in, numbering them in priority if they want to be in more than one group, and then fold the form and hand it in. Since the number of self-referrals tends to be high, be sure to tell the children that not everyone may be in a group right away. Assure them, however, that groups will be offered according to time and need.

Broader Community. Sharing information about the group program with parents, professionals, and other concerned adults at a community forum will lead to referrals from the broader community. For example, once therapists and social workers from treatment centers and mental health agencies know about your group program, they will be able to refer some of their clients to it.

When it comes to referrals, the rule of thumb is "the broader the referral network, the better." The broader the referral network, the better the chance at-risk children will be reached and helped.

Screening Candidates

No matter how children are referred for membership in a *Building Trust, Making Friends* group, each candidate should be screened individually before you grant membership. The screening process consists of a brief interview that details demographic factors, the child's adjustment and attitude toward school, and the child's family or living situation. (See the Screening Interview Outline on page 230.) If the child is self-referred, and if you or other group leaders have no knowledge of the child's particular family stress, screening will help gather specific information about it.

During the screening interview, make the child as comfortable as possible, acknowledge loyalty to the family, stress confidentiality, and reassure the child that such questioning will not take place in front of other children. Ask respectfully for specific information about the family stress. Listen carefully to the child's reasons for self-referral, then use your best judgment about whether or not to include the child in the group. For example, a child may refer himself or herself to a group dealing with chemical dependence because his or her parents smoke cigarettes and the child has learned that tobacco contains the drug nicotine. Whether to include this child depends on the child's adjustment and on your sense of the needs and priorities of other group members, the school itself, and the administration.

If you know about the family stress of a particular candidate, and the child is in denial (therefore, generally not self-referred), there's no need to break that denial during the screening interview. Simply help the child see that being part of the group is a way to learn what the fictional characters—who will be introduced in the group—learned about the issues in their families.

If you feel that the child belongs in a group, discuss the group process, including group format and session topics, with the child. Describing the format will prepare the child for what will happen in group and will reassure the child about the safety of the group. Show the child a copy of the Group Rules Contract (see page 168). Explain the rules and tell the child that to be in the group he or she must attend every group session and keep all the rules. If you wish, tell the child that at the first group session all group members will be asked to sign a copy of the Group Rules Contract. This process sets the stage for good behavior during the group sessions.

The prospect of screening every group candidate individually may seem a bit daunting. But such screening isn't just for your sake and the program's sake. It's also a valuable experience for the child. The screening may also serve as a case-finding procedure, during which cases of alcohol and other drug experimentation or sexual or physical abuse may come to light and can be dealt with properly. Naturally, cases of sexual or physical abuse should be reported immediately to appropriate authorities. The screening may reveal that the child needs a group experience regarding another family issue. If such is the case, you can make the appropriate referral.

Acquiring Informed Parental Consent

To ensure a group's integrity and success, you need to acquire consent from the parents whose children are candidates for group membership. Procedures for acquiring parental consent must consider the children's needs, the parents' rights to privacy, the school's desire to help its students, and the provisions of the law so as to avoid any legal action being taken against the school.

The simplest way to get informed consent is to have the school mail a letter to the parents of all prospective group members that clearly but simply:

- describes the program and group process
- encourages parents to allow their child to receive the services the program and group can provide
- informs parents that they must contact the school if they do not want their child to participate (see the Parental Consent Letter on page 229).

If you feel that parents will be resistant, visit with them personally to talk about it. Take along the toy animal you will use in group and share with the parents what it will learn in a fun and nonjudgmental way from Mrs. Owl. Explain the group format and progression of themes. Explain that you're not looking for pathology or problems, but rather are hoping to correct misconceptions and to teach coping skills. Once the program is explained well to parents, few are likely to refuse permission for their child to take part.

There will be times when you, another group leader, or school staff member will identify a particular child who could benefit by participating in a group, but whose parents refuse to allow it. If you've clearly explained the purpose and format of the program to the parents and they still don't want their child involved, there are still two ways you can help the child. First, make sure that the child is present for any in-school presentation about the program, either one you offer as a recruitment tool or one that students themselves might provide (for example, the presentation provided by the optional Session 10). An at-risk child can begin to integrate facts, concepts, and specific skills even when the presentation is brief. Second, you can refer that child to the school counseling services for individual assistance. Some counselors modify this program to use with children individually. Finally, remember, this program is not the only help available to at-risk children.

Forming and Scheduling the Groups

You know from your own experience that the best groups—of any kind—are made up of different individuals with varying temperaments and personalities. The same is true for the groups in this program. To the best of your ability, see to it that groups are a mix of children who are outgoing, shy, talkative, quiet, boys, girls, and so on. However, because of children's developmental differences, you must be careful about mixing children from different grade levels into a single group. It's best not to have a spread larger than one grade level. Kindergarten and first-grade groups can be effective, but kindergarten to second grade is probably too great a spread.

Group size is also determined by the age of group members. Groups of younger children should be smaller, since they require more time, help, and individual attention. To determine group size, follow the guidelines below:

- kindergarten, first, and second grade—four children per group
- third, fourth, and fifth grade—six children per group
- sixth grade and up—seven to eight children per group

For rich group dynamics and useful interactions, eight seems to be the maximum number of participants for the structured groups of this program. When the group size extends beyond eight, the level of individual attention and sharing diminishes. If you find that more children want to participate, offer more groups as it becomes possible to do so.

The location, size, and atmosphere of a group's meeting room are very important in establishing a safe, welcoming space for children to open up and take risks. Generally, classrooms aren't the most satisfactory places for group meetings; they're almost always too large and are filled with too many distractions. Ideally, the meeting room needs to be small, comfortable, and quiet, a place where interruptions and potential distractions are minimal. Privacy is essential so youngsters won't be afraid that others outside the room can see or overhear them. Seating each child at a table will help avoid fidgety behavior and simplify the drawing and writing activities.

Survey your school facility for a good place for group meetings. Obviously, such a space is often at a premium in a school setting, so remember that your most important considerations are privacy, quiet, and regular availability.

Besides matters of space, scheduling must also deal with matters of time. The group sessions are designed to last approximately 45 minutes. Plan to hold them on a weekly basis so that the children have time to integrate the insight and support gained from each session. Weekly sessions are also less likely to interfere with the children's studies and other activities. Try to schedule group meetings for elementary-aged children on the same day, at the same time, and in the same place each week. Although you'll want to make the meeting place and day consistent for middle school groups, you may rotate meeting times so that the children won't miss instruction in the same subject each week. For example, for the first week, schedule the group to meet during the first instructional hour; for the second week, schedule it during the second instructional hour, and so on.

In all matters of scheduling, administrative support is an invaluable aid to help foster teacher cooperation in releasing students from regular classes. Remember, however, that cooperation is a two-way street. Let children and teachers know that students participate in the group on the condition that they make up all missed work. Likewise, give teachers a schedule of group meetings so that they'll know in advance what class a child will miss, won't plan field trips or tests for those times, and can make arrangements for the child to make up missed school work.

Assuring Group Confidentiality

Confidentiality is the cornerstone of safe and supportive groups. To share problems and deep feelings, the children must know that what they say will be kept in confidence. Experts have pointed out that at-risk children are very reluctant to reveal family problems. For example, often there are unspoken rules in an at-risk family: "Don't talk; don't trust; don't feel" (Black 1981). It's important to realize that the children will not open up if they think that what they share will become common knowledge around school. Group confidentiality therefore, must be an absolute guarantee.

This program's group model not only guarantees confidentiality but also adds a "plus" to it. Families are accepted and valued in the group, never condemned. The children have opportunities to share feelings and to self-disclose as they choose, all the while remaining loyal to their families. Although they have many opportunities to take an active part in every group session, if they choose to pass, they may, and the group leader respects their decision. Meanwhile, the group leaders provide a corrective experience for the children. By their warm acceptance and nonjudgmental attitudes, they build an atmosphere of trust. Through each session's bibliotherapy, they talk openly about what happens in families. As the children grow more secure, they feel safe to self-disclose and identify and share feelings, which the group leaders help them express in appropriate ways. Remember, however, that self-disclosure is not the goal of the group. Children who never say a word in group can still benefit.

In setting up groups, therefore, take extra care to assure and protect confidentiality. The children must realize that outside of the group sessions they may not discuss who else is in their group or what they say. Children can, however, discuss the facts and information they learn during group. The group leaders must remember their responsibilities as well. Except in cases where the law requires such revelation (for example, where a group leader suspects that a child is being physically or sexually abused), it is inappropriate for a group leader to reveal to others anything a child may share. It's a good idea, therefore, to inform the children of this at the very first session.

But what about teachers in the school? Don't they have a right to know when a child will miss class because of his or her participation in a group? Yes, they do. But isn't this a breach of confidentiality? No, not at all. To help maintain confidentiality, you need only inform teachers that a group is part of the school counseling program and that the children in it are going to learn basic facts about alcohol and other drugs, family violence, or divorce. For even further confidentiality, you might give the groups simple, generic names. For example, call a group for elementary-aged students that focuses on chemical dependence the "Star Group" or a group for middle school students that focuses on family violence the "Moon Group." That way, neither school staff nor anyone else (except specific group members) will know what kind of group a child is in or what the child's specific problem(s) might be. Teachers will only know that one or more of their students are taking part in a group.

Self-disclosing by Leaders

Since the children aren't required or asked to self-disclose, should group leaders self-disclose? If used correctly, self-disclosure can be a useful group technique with children in the fourth grade and up. Even so, leaders should be very cautious and think carefully before self-disclosing. Sharing facts about one's personal life is appropriate only if it's positive role modeling or if it will help illustrate a point effectively. However, leaders should never employ self-disclosure for purposes of eliciting the same from children, nor should they use the group for personal therapy. For example, leaders must not express feelings or share experiences that they haven't adequately resolved or dealt with themselves. From a developmental perspective, self-disclosure is a poor device to use with younger children (grades K-3), who are too egocentric to benefit from such information. Group leaders steer a surer course by focusing on the curriculum and listening to what the children have to say. If you're ever in doubt whether to self-disclose, a good rule of thumb is to trust your doubt and don't.

Role Modeling by Leaders

Although group leaders should make their own decision regarding self-disclosure, the program does ask leaders to share of themselves several times during each group session. Leaders act as role models for important components. Leaders begin the go-arounds for the feelings check-in, the affirmation, and the closing activity of each session. During the feelings check-in, leaders act as role models by sharing appropriate feelings and facts, such as, "I'm glad to see you" or "I'm feeling sad because my dog died." During the affirmation, leaders model what it means to take a positive attitude, choose helpful ways to choose and express anger, or have a repertoire of coping strategies. Overall, it's important to follow the rule of thumb described above. Never share a feeling or issue that you have not dealt with or resolved adequately. Doing so would be poor role modeling.

Following Up Group Participation

Some children who participate in the program's groups will require further services. If, for instance, children have severe behavior problems, it's unlikely that one group experience will enable them to deal much differently or much more effectively with the stress in their lives. Realizing this, be sure to make further help available. That help can come in the form of individual, group, or system follow-up.

Individual Follow-up. A counselor can continue to see the children individually. Follow-up counseling sessions can help them learn to integrate and use in their own lives the concepts and skills the group presented.

Group Follow-up. For children with serious behavior problems, participating in other group experiences can be very beneficial. For example, elementary-aged children who have participated in the group Peter the Puppy Talks About Chemical Dependence in the Family may still have difficulty dealing with or expressing their anger in helpful ways. Such children could benefit from taking part in the group Della the Dinosaur Talks About Violence and Anger Management.

Getting children to participate in another group is usually easy, since they enjoy the familiarity, consistency, and predictability of the group format. In fact, most children who participate in more than one group find that they're old hands at the group exercises, and they like meeting Mrs. Owl again.

Be aware, however, that children should probably not participate in more than one group at a time. Instead, encourage them to spread their participation over one or two years.

System Follow-up. Children with particularly intense behavior problems may require the services of a schoolwide helping plan as follow-up to their participation in a group. Such services can include any or all of the following: (1) individual counseling; (2) successive group experiences; (3) a proactive schoolwide plan for anger management (see the Background and Guidelines section for Session 7 on page 108); (4) participation in a peer counseling program; and (5) frequent consultation between counselor and teachers and other school staff to enable them to help children use coping techniques, such as the centering exercises and anger management. Of course, recognize that you may want or need to refer a child or family for outside therapy.

Using the Program in Guidance Counseling

Guidance counselors and other professionals have found this program's centering exercises, anger management plan, and basic facts very useful not only when working with children in groups but when working with children individually as well. Because the program's concepts, including the basic education about the issues and the correction of children's misconceptions, are clear and easily identifiable, they enhance assessment skills. They also empower counselors in individual counseling with children. Instead of just discussing feelings with the children, counselors can impart information and correct misconceptions. Also, the skills presented in the program are effective techniques that children learn, master, and use.

Guidance counselors who have led program groups have been able to teach centering exercises and anger management plans and use the basic facts and coping strategy scenarios in classroom guidance. They report that children who have participated in this program's groups are usually actively involved in the classroom discussion, which reveals that children truly do integrate crucial concepts presented by the program (for example, "Divorce is never the child's fault"). Counselors generally report that leading these groups gives them a sense of greater competence, effectiveness, and empowerment.

Using the Program in Family Therapy

The program's group model works not only in schools, mental health facilities, and treatment centers. It also works well in family therapy with families experiencing chemical dependence, divorce, or family violence, or with families in which children exhibit aggressive behavior.

By using the program's format and stories (bibliotherapy), therapists can help family members become aware of and learn the facts about whatever issue has brought them to therapy. They can see the impact the issue has made on the family and their feelings about it. The program can help the family with anger management, coping strategies, setting personal goals, and developing a support system. During group sessions, the helping professional in the stories (bibliotherapy) serves as a role model for parents.

Just as the program corrects misconceptions for children, it also corrects them for parents. For instance, a mother who engages in long-term conflict with an ex-spouse may come to see that it's important for her children to be friendly with both parents, and she will then lessen her part in the conflict. Or, a father whose spouse is chemically dependent might come to understand that his wife has a disease, that alcohol or another drug is causing the changes in her behavior, and that her problems aren't his fault or his problems. Likewise, parents who express anger by yelling can learn to use—and benefit from—the program's centering exercises and anger management steps. Finally, all parents can benefit by learning that feelings should be identified, accepted, and shared in helpful ways.

****

The *Building Trust, Making Friends* program was developed for caring professionals like you who are concerned about at-risk children. It will help you enhance the emotional growth, safety, and self-esteem of these children. It will also give at-risk children the chance to obtain the skills they need to maintain their physical and emotional health and to correct any misconceptions they may have developed. Living healthfully and well is a risky business. All children, especially at-risk children, deserve the chance to take that risk.

Part Two

Group Guide for Della the Dinosaur Talks About Violence and Anger Management

Chapter 1: Issues Affecting Children from Violent Families

The Influence of the Violent Home

In today's world of accelerated pace, overwhelming pressure, and financial strain, the problem of domestic violence has become rampant. Its effects devastate not only the participants, but their children as well. Violence comes in many forms: physical, emotional, sexual, and social. If violence is physical and escalates to a high enough degree, it may become fatal, ending in murder or suicide.

As someone who works with children, you're well aware that parents have a major influence on a child's life. Parents' views, behaviors, traditions, and mores shape the growing child. Thus, it should come as no surprise to learn that studies have shown that children growing up in violent homes frequently learn to behave violently. This is particularly true with boys. Statistics also indicate that 80 percent of adults who exhibit violent behavior were either abused or witnessed abuse in their homes during childhood. Boys often become violent toward the women with whom they are most closely bonded: mothers, sisters, and eventually, wives. Conversely, girls from violent homes may take on the role of victim or become similarly violent themselves. No matter their age—and even though they witness the people they love most inflicting or being the victims of violence—children growing up in violent homes are "taught" that violence is an effective mechanism for gaining control over others.

Violent homes frequently harbor other problems, including chemical dependence, that exacerbate an already traumatizing situation and impose further debilitating effects upon the children, who must live with their consequences. Problems like these reinforce the need for groups designed to help children at-risk due to violence in the home.

The primary goal of the Della the Dinosaur Group is to help children recognize that they are not the cause of the violence or abuse in their home, and that they can neither control nor cure it. At the same time, the group helps children discover mechanisms to protect and help themselves. It also helps them learn techniques to cope with a very painful situation. That way, these children have a much better chance of growing up safe, healthy, and refusing to use violence as a way of expressing and dealing with the difficult situations in their lives.

Abusive and neglectful behavior, however, is not a chronic disease, one that never goes away. In fact, it is not a disease at all, but learned behavior. As such, it can be unlearned and replaced by nonabusive behavior (Sanford 1990). This is emphasized because children who have been victims of violence are frequently categorized as "damaged goods" who believe that they are unworthy human beings and are certain to be traumatized forever. These children need to realize that although they have been hurt, they are not forever disabled. Learning to cope, leave their past behind, and discover new life skills can help them see themselves as whole and capable human beings.

Too often abusive people are excused by blaming an abusive childhood for their behavior. They are made "forever victims." By blaming persons' violent behavior on the past, their present and future are limited. Their free will and their right and responsibility for choosing their behavior is taken away. They are denied the hope and health that by right belongs to them.

One of the goals of this program is to minimize the self-fulfilling prophecy that children who experience abuse, either directly or vicariously, will become abusers themselves. With proper education and steadfast support, the cycle can be broken. However, children must first learn that they are not responsible for the family violence, regardless of whether it's adult-to-adult or adult-to-child.

What Children Learn in Violent Homes

To grow and blossom, children need security, warmth, nurturance, and guidance. Childhood should be a time of no-risk dependence on others, a time when children feel love and acceptance with no strings attached, a time when children get their needs met sufficiently to enter into adulthood with a sense of internal security and trust.

Children who grow up in violent families often don't get these needs met in healthy ways. They emerge into adulthood with serious detrimental dependencies. They may have a sense of incompleteness and mistrust, and may believe that there is something intrinsically wrong with them. They often feel a great deal of shame, that they're not okay, and that they're powerless—especially powerless to change themselves. These children, therefore, develop a strong need for some kind of security outside themselves, which can lead to the vicious cycle of co-dependence and other addictive lifestyles.

A number of experts have written about the characteristics of abnormal family systems and their impact on children. Friel and Friel (1988) write about the concept of *vicarious abuse,* which has influenced the approach taken in *Della the Dinosaur Talks About Violence and Anger Management*. Vicarious abuse refers to the phenomenon that when children witness the abuse of anyone else, they also become victims of that abuse. This can take the form of children's feeling guilty that they were treated "better" than the person who has been abused; or children may feel more powerful because they were treated "better." Children may also feel frightened that they may be the abuser's next victim; or they may fear for their safety should something happen to their primary caretaker.

Vicarious abuse is just as painful, hurtful, and harmful as other kinds of abuse. It's important not to discount the impact that vicarious abuse can have on children. Experts remind us that vicarious abuse damages children—causing "persistent negative effects" of living with trauma—not so much by what actually took place (the violent behavior) but by what *did not* take place afterwards. Very often when children reveal their experience of violent events, they are disbelieved, shamed, threatened into silence, told that the violence never took place or that their perception of it is incorrect, or, worst of all, their disclosure precipitates punishment. When these things happen, the effects of the original trauma are compounded.

Children, then, are frequently left on their own to try and make sense of an abnormal situation. They often end up repressing the event: "That really didn't happen." Or, they engage in psychic numbing: "This really isn't painful." Children should not be so abandoned. Caring adults must not discount the impact that vicarious abuse has on them. Instead, they must help them survive the aftermath of traumatic events by providing them with a sense of safety and well-being. When children who are victims of violence—even vicarious abuse—are treated realistically, compassionately, and protectively, they will experience such care as much more meaningful than the trauma they've suffered. Children can withstand a lot with the help of others. But if children's thoughts or feelings are denied, that denial can cause as much pain as did the original trauma itself.

Children who live in families where there is direct or vicarious abuse may:

1. Have a poor self-image; feel that they don't matter or that there is something wrong with them.
2. Need individual attention.
3. Need to express frustration and anger.
4. Have unattended educational and medical needs.
5. Need to succeed and experience success—to do something right.
6. Need to know that they have rights, too; those with poor self-esteem may not realize that it's okay to say no to adults.
7. Have hampered emotional, physical, or sexual development.

Adults often don't realize that children generally learn to obey commands through experience. Children who live in families with violence or who have been exposed to inconsistent parenting may be convinced that most adults do not mean well. If an adult, such as a teacher, makes a request of these children, they may not comply, because they are unconvinced that compliance is in their own best interest. These children have not learned to trust adults. Only by teaching children that they don't cause, can't control, and can't cure the family's problem (of violence), and by being consistent, predictable, and nonjudgmental, can children who live in families with violence be empowered to make a difference in their own lives.

The Role of the Group

Since children who experience parental violence are at risk for difficulties in their behavioral, social, and emotional adjustment, they are prime candidates to participate in a small group, school-based, prevention and intervention program. Groups are ideal settings in which children can learn the facts about both helpful and harmful ways to express feelings, discover the common conflicts for children from families with violence, and develop the skills they need to live healthy lives. Supported by others in the group, children can more easily come to understand and accept these issues, which is necessary if they are to grasp how parental violence affects their families and themselves.

More than being settings for sharing facts, however, groups are settings that provide opportunities for children to share feelings in a nonjudgmental atmosphere of mutual respect. Groups serve to reduce the isolation members feel and to offer them needed support and affirmation. Groups help children discover that feelings are not right or wrong—"good or bad"—but just *are* (Typpo and Hastings, 1984). Groups also give children opportunities to learn from each other's experiences, to accept that violence does affect them, and to recognize that asking for what they need is not only okay, but essential and healthy. Groups seek to help youngsters build self-esteem through a better understanding of themselves, their parents, and healthy functioning both in school and in other areas of their lives. Possibly, the greatest gift these children need to receive is the chance to have fun. The group experience can make this opportunity a reality.

In summary, the role of the group is to help children from families with violence:

1. Reduce their isolating belief that they are the only ones who have such trauma in their lives.
2. Identify and correct some of their common misconceptions (such as, they've caused the violence; they can control the violence).
3. Identify and validate the feelings common to such children.

4. Learn effective coping strategies to deal with their feelings, for example, anger management.
5. Learn coping strategies to avoid taking sides in parental conflicts and to avoid assuming parental responsibilities.
6. Learn that they can ask for help for themselves and can take care of themselves.
7. Relax and have fun in a nurturing and conflict-free environment.

Understanding Children's Developmental Characteristics

How you help children from at-risk families depends on how open they are to your help. This program has been carefully designed to be developmentally appropriate for children in grades K-6. The following developmental characteristics were determining factors in the formation of this group model program.

K-3 Children. Children in the lower elementary grades (ages five to seven) have a high activity level and are generally openly affectionate. By age seven, they have developed a sense of shame, are more careful in their work habits, have lost some of their self-confidence, and require the positive feedback of others. As to value development, these children experience difficulty distinguishing between actions and consequences. They believe that punishment automatically follows wrongdoing. And they accept the authority of the family without much question. According to Piaget (1928), children between the ages of four and seven are ruled by perception. They believe that what they see *is*. They reach conclusions based on impressions and judgments, not words. For example, if they perceive a cow as purple, they believe all cows are purple. They have a difficult time distinguishing between fantasy and reality. They express their fears and anxieties not through language, but through symbolic play. In their play, for example, they may act out scenarios between powerful heroes and villains, or they may act out concerns by playing "school" or dolls.

Grades 3-6. Children in grades 3-6 are judgmental and dramatic. Since they're concerned with what their parents think of them , they stick close to get clues to their parents' reactions to them. By fourth grade, most children accept responsibility for their actions and are able to distinguish between wrongdoing and its underlying motive. They begin forming close, same-sex friendships. Fifth grade is the highpoint of childhood. Children experience more self-acceptance, are better at sports, and enjoy organized group activities and secret clubs. Fifth-graders generally enjoy family members and family outings. They perceive parental warnings as genuine expressions of concern and appreciate them, even if they don't always heed them.

In regard to value development, children in grades 3-6 shift from judging actions in terms of their seriousness to judging them in terms of their motivations. These children are particularly influenced by the behavior of parents. For example, when parents model the behaviors they desire from their children, such as not smoking, the children are more likely to follow that behavior. These children are fascinated with how the world works. They're beginning to think logically. They're able to put things into categories and to realize that an item can be in more than one group at a time. For example, they can understand that their mother is also a daughter. They're learning to operate according to rules, such as those found in arithmetic and reading. These children also love board games, sports games, and self-made games that have clearly stated rules.

The session plans detailed in the next chapter were designed with these developmental characteristics in mind.

Chapter 2: Session Plans

Della the Dinosaur Talks About Violence and Anger Management educates and empowers children in grades K-6 from families with violence to deal effectively with their feelings and discover the coping skills they need to survive and remain healthy.

This guide contains eleven group-session plans for facilitating a support group for elementary school-aged children:

Session 1: Della the Dinosaur Talks About Feelings

Session 2: Della the Dinosaur Talks About Violence

Session 3: Della the Dinosaur Talks About Violence in Her Family

Session 4: Della the Dinosaur Meets Mrs. Owl

Session 5: Della the Dinosaur Learns About Feelings

Session 6: Della the Dinosaur Talks About Anger

Session 7: Della the Dinosaur Learns to Manage Anger

Session 8: Della the Dinosaur Learns Other Coping Strategies

Session 9: Della the Dinosaur Learns How to Take Care of Herself

Session 10: Group Presentation—*Optional*

Session 11: Della the Dinosaur Says Goodbye

Each plan begins with the *Objectives* section. This section sets a clear direction for the group session.

The *Session at a Glance* section outlines the session and includes suggested times for each of the plan's components. If you carefully go over the plan in advance, this section can serve as a quick reference as you move through the session.

The *Preparation* section, which follows, lists materials needed and gives directions for getting ready for the session. (Note: When directions in this section call for copies of various materials, these may be found in blackline master form in Part Three of this manual, "Support Materials," pages 165-232. One such set of materials is the Basic Facts Worksheets, which will be used in every session. If you wish, when you copy these sheets for the children, you can mount them on construction paper for a special touch, which the children value. Another set of materials is the Basic Facts Posters. These posters make excellent teaching aids when copied and laminated or made into transparencies. You will need to make copies of these posters to use as you present the sessions.)

To assure the best results in leading the sessions, you'll want to find appealing and cuddly stuffed toy animals to portray Della the Dinosaur and Mrs. Owl. Securing a stuffed toy dinosaur is generally no problem, but finding a toy stuffed owl or owl puppet may prove difficult. If you have problems, you can order one from the following address:

Country Critters	or from	Made in Kanas
217 Neosho		Box D
Burlington, KS 66839		Burlington, KS 66839
316-364-8623		800-728-1332

The *Background and Guidelines* section will enrich your understanding of the session's focus and key concepts, as well as guide you through the plan itself. For the most part, the plan's structure follows the same format for each session and unfolds in three stages. *Beginning the Session* is the first stage and includes a review of group rules, a centering exercise, a feelings check-in (Session 1 substitutes an ice-breaker), and a review of basic facts (starting with Session 2). The second stage, *Exploring the Story*, includes the story, discussion, activity, and basic facts. *Wrapping Up* is the third stage and includes a repetition of the centering exercise, an affirmation, and a closing activity.

This format provides the children with a total experience that is structured as well as welcoming and accepting, instructional as well as creative and enjoyable, challenging as well as affirming and fun. Since the format remains the same for each session, it meets the needs at-risk children have for structure, consistency, predictability, and fun. Each group session is designed to take approximately 45 minutes, but can be shortened or extended to meet local circumstances.

If you are a new group leader, you should follow up each session by filling out a copy of the Process and Progress Form (see page 225). This form enables you to evaluate the session's effectiveness and to track the children's progress. It also serves as a useful tool when training new group leaders. If you are an experienced leader, you may follow up each session by filling out the Progress Notes (see page 226). No matter what your experience, it's a good idea to keep some form of notes on each session.

You may feel that certain sessions in this curriculum contain enough information to be scheduled over two meeting times. You may find this especially true for Session 4. If you have the time, you may simply follow the session plan as given, but only present half of the plan during one session time. Also, occasionally a session may offer an alternative suggestion to the given activity. This allows you more choice and flexibility in leading your group. It also can help you tailor the sessions to the particular needs and idiosyncrasies of the group members.

Session 10 is an *optional* session. Its structure varies from the other sessions in that group members will present facts they've learned to an invited audience. You may or may not choose to involve the children in this session. If you decide to use the session, know that its format and method of presentation will vary from group to group depending on the group members' developmental levels and the makeup of the invited audience. For this session to be successful, you should schedule *two meeting times* to present it. Use the first time period as a practice session to help the children decide on the type and content of their presentation, to make all necessary preparations, and to practice their presentation. Use the second time period to conduct the actual session. Again, to guarantee success, plan ahead for Session 10.

These session plans have been carefully crafted and tested. Use them carefully, creatively, and confidently. Everything you need is here.

Session 1: Della the Dinosaur Talks About Feelings

Objectives

To help the children:

- recognize that everyone has feelings and that all feelings are normal
- discover and describe one harmful and one helpful way to express anger

Session at a Glance

1. Welcome and Group Rules (Group Rules Contract)—4 minutes
2. Centering exercise: "Breathing Through Your Feet"—4 minutes
3. Ice-breaker—6 minutes
4. The Story: meet Della the Dinosaur; make Della the Dinosaur puppets (Activity Sheet 1); share story—8 minutes
5. Discussion—5 minutes
6. Activity: draw and share a picture of someone who is angry (Activity Sheet 2)—7 minutes
7. Basic Facts: (Worksheet 1) read aloud; discuss; fill in blanks; read aloud together—2 minutes
8. Centering Exercise: repeat "Breathing Through Your Feet"—4 minutes
9. Affirmation: share something you liked about the group—3 minutes
10. Closing: have a silent wish and squeeze—2 minutes

Preparation

- Choose an appealing and cuddly stuffed toy animal (brontosaurus) to portray Della the Dinosaur. Try to have the toy resemble the finger puppet pictured on Activity Sheet 1.
- Make a copy of each of the eighteen Basic Facts Posters (see pages 203-220). If possible, laminate the posters or make transparencies. You'll need Basic Facts Posters 1 and 2 in this session.
- Make a copy of the Group Rules Contract (see page 168), one for each child. To save time at the copy machine, also make each child a copy of the feeling wheel, each of the eleven Activity Sheets and the nine Basic Facts Worksheets now. (Note: If your group is made up of kindergartners, first graders, or children from a special education population, you may wish to use copies of the Basic Facts Worksheets with Answers Dotted In on pages 192-202.)
- To save time during the session, pre-cut and paste the Della the Dinosaur puppets (from Activity Sheet 1) for the children.
- Copy the group rules onto a large sheet of posterboard that you can display in the group meeting space during this and future sessions.
- Have a large manila folder for each child; print the child's name on the folder.
- Include in each child's folder:

  - a 3" x 5" lined index card

  - a copy of the Group Rules Contract, Activity Sheet 1 ("Della the Dinosaur Puppet"), Activity Sheet 2 ("This Person Is Angry"), and Basic Facts Worksheet 1
- Have the folder, a pencil, and crayons or markers at each student's place. Make sure the crayons include a red, purple, blue, and yellow color.
- Make a poster to use during the session's Ice-breaker. On newsprint, list the following questions:

  - What is your name?

  - How old are you?

  - What grade are you in?

  - What neighborhood do you live in?

  - Who lives in your house?

  - What's your favorite food?

  - What's your favorite TV show?
- Read through the session plan before meeting.

Background and Guidelines

As you present the session, understand that children are often unaware of their feelings, and thus are unable to put them into words. Instead, children either act out their feelings or pretend that they don't have them. Part of the therapeutic process is to help the children identify, accept, and appropriately express their feelings.

Since this curriculum deals primarily with the feeling of anger, it's important for you to have dealt with any personal issues surrounding anger. You must be able to accept anger as a normal and healthy feeling, and to choose helpful ways to express angry feelings.

Be careful to be nonjudgmental as you talk about people who use violence to express anger. Help the children see that such people are not bad people. Rather, they are choosing harmful ways to express their anger. Assure the children that there are other choices available. Knowing this helps the youngsters feel accepted and willing to trust. It also helps them avoid feeling disloyal to their families. Emphasizing the *choice* to use violence and labeling *that* as the problem helps the children begin to realize that *they* have choices about how they will express *their* feelings.

Overall, your task is to empower the children: to help them see that they can learn the facts about families who use violence to express anger; to help them learn to recognize and deal with the effects of such violence on their families and themselves; to help them see that they can choose helpful ways to express their feelings; and to help them learn and practice coping strategies that will help them take good care of themselves. The structure and format of this session and those that follow are designed to help you do this. It's left to you to add the important human touch that makes for trust, comfort, understanding, cohesiveness, and fun.

Beginning the Session

Group Rules

Prepare the room by placing the folders, pencils, and crayons at each student's place. Welcome the children and have them sit at a table. Explain that this is the Della the Dinosaur Group. Everyone in the group will have lots of chances to have fun, learn about feelings, especially anger, and find new ways to feel better and to take care of themselves.

Explain to the children that they will use their folders every time they meet and that everything they need will be in these folders. Ask the children to open their folders and take out a pencil and their copy of the Group Rules Contract. Meanwhile, display the poster you made listing the group rules. Tell the children that like every group—use examples of groups like Scouts, band, and secret clubs—their group has rules. For the group to work well, everyone needs to keep the rules. Even though the children will have encountered these rules in their screening interview, take a moment to go through them now to check for understanding:

1. I will keep what we talk about private.
   We call this confidentiality.
2. I will stay in my seat.
3. I will keep my hands to myself.
4. I will wait for my turn to talk,
   and I will listen carefully when others talk.
5. I won't tease or put other people down.
6. I can "pass" during go-arounds.
7. I will come to every group session.
8. I will make up any class work I miss.

Draw attention to the first rule regarding confidentiality. Remind the children that no one will know what they share in group, with one exception. If they share in group that someone is hurting them or touching them inappropriately, you will have to report that information to help them stay safe. Once the children understand this and the other rules, have them sign and date their Group Rules Contracts. If group members are kindergartners or first graders, be ready to offer assistance.

Have the children place their contracts in their folders. Explain that they will be using the folders to hold all their group work, that each week new materials will be added to the folders, and that you will keep the folders safe until the end of the group's sessions when the children can take them home. Tell the children that they can decorate their folders at the beginning of each session, while waiting for the session to begin.

Keep the group rules poster and display it every time the group meets.

Centering Exercise

The first time you lead a centering exercise, it may feel odd to be directing the children to go into a "dark and scary place." Know that the goal of the exercise is not to frighten the children nor to get them *into* a "dark and scary place." Rather, as children from violent homes, they are already *in* a dark and scary place. The intent of the exercise is to teach the children some skills to get *out*.

Since most of the children will not have encountered an exercise like this before, give them—and yourself—time to get into it. Begin by inviting the children to relax and by telling them that the name of the exercise is "Breathing Through Your Feet."

Close your eyes. Imagine that you are all alone in a dark place. It's kind of scary there and hard to breathe. You can get out of that scary, dark place. All you have to know is a secret. I know the secret, and I'll share it with you.

The secret is breathing through your feet!

Imagine that you have tiny holes all over the bottom of your feet. Your shoes are dotted with tiny holes, too. Now, breathe air up through those holes—all the way up to your ankles, right on to your knees, past your waist, right through your stomach, and into your lungs. Hold that air in your lungs. Feel how refreshing it is. Now push the air all the way back down your body—out of your lungs and down through your stomach, past your waist and on to your knees, all the way down to your ankles, and out through your feet.

(Lead the children through this process five times, for a total of five deep breaths; give directions softly; make sure that the children inhale and exhale evenly and slowly. Finally, conclude the exercise by saying:)

You've learned the secret of breathing through your feet. This secret can give you power. Whenever you feel scared or find yourself in a scary place, you can use breathing through your feet to get to a safe place in your mind. Imagine that you are in a safe place right now.

(Adapted from *The Stress-Proof Child*, by Saunders and Remsberg, 1984.)

Ice-breaker

Involve the children in an ice-breaker. Have the children get their index cards from their folders. Display the poster you made prior to the session that asks the children to list their name, age, grade, neighborhood where they live, who lives in their house, a favorite food, and a favorite TV show. Have the children write their answers to the questions. Share the information in a go-around. To role model for the children, begin by sharing the information about yourself (you can pass on your age if you wish). Then have each group member share. (Note: For younger children, you may have to ask the questions and get responses orally.)

This safe and nonthreatening activity helps the children feel comfortable about sharing information, and introduces them to the go-around technique.

Exploring the Story

The Story

To get the youngsters ready for the story, show them the cuddly stuffed toy animal (dinosaur) you acquired and introduce it as Della the Dinosaur. Explain that Della will be with them every time they meet to have fun and to share information with them. Tell the children that each of them will have a chance to hold Della during their time together, but that they can also make their own Della the Dinosaur puppet. Have the youngsters take out the pre-cut and pasted Della the Dinosaur puppet patterns (Activity Sheet 1) and crayons. Invite the children to color the puppets. Then, settle the children to hear a story. Using the cuddly toy dinosaur, have *Della* tell the following:

Hi! My name is Della the Dinosaur. I want to talk to you about something that's kind of scary, but that's really important. I want to talk to you about violence in the family.

There are lots of different kinds of families. And everybody in these families has lots of different kinds of feelings. Family members can feel sad, glad, scared, or angry. They may even feel more than one feeling at a time.

But guess what? Family members don't always show their feelings or deal with them in the same way. Some try to pretend that they don't have any feelings at all. Others try to swallow down their feelings—maybe because they don't know what to do with them. Or, they might be afraid to express them. Some family members choose to express ("express" means "show") their feelings in helpful ways, but others choose to express their feelings in harmful ways.

One of the feelings that people and dinosaurs have is anger. Anger is a feeling that has been given a bad name. Some people think that anger is a bad feeling to have. Actually, anger is a very normal feeling. Most people like you and most dinosaurs like me feel angry as often as twelve to fourteen times a day. Anger can be a positive force if we use our anger to work for us. We can use our anger to help us play sports better. We can use our anger to get us ready to really get started on our homework. We can even use our anger to control ourselves. We can use our anger in positive, powerful ways. We can also express our anger in *helpful* ways.

What gets people like you and dinosaurs like me into trouble is when we choose to express our anger in *harmful* ways—in violent ways. You see, it's never okay for a dinosaur, a child, or a grown-up to express anger in a way that hurts themselves or anyone else.

Let me tell you about some helpful ways and harmful ways of expressing anger.

One day my best friend, Dinah Dimetrodon, called me a nasty name. She called me "scaleface." I was so angry that I smacked her with my tail. That time, I chose to express my anger in a *harmful* way.

One time, Trevor Tyrannosaurus pushed me while we were standing in the lunch line at school. I felt really angry, but I took a deep breath and counted to ten. Then I politely asked Trevor to please stop pushing. I chose to express my anger in a *helpful* way that time.

Once, in class, Joanna and Megan, the Stegosaurus twins who sit in front of me, were whispering to each other. But the teacher thought that I was the one who was talking, so she put my name on the board. I was so angry that I didn't do my work for the rest of the day. That was a *harmful* way to express my anger.

One day, I really wanted to go out and play with the other dinosaurs, but my mom wouldn't let me go. I felt angry about it, but I decided to go into my room and tell my toy people how angry I felt. That was a *helpful* way to express my anger.

The next time *you* feel angry, remember it's okay to feel that way. Just remember to try to use your anger to work for you or to *express* your anger in a *helpful* way. Bye now. See you soon.

Discussion

Lead the group in a discussion to help the children better understand the facts—the key concepts—the story presented. In your discussion, allow the children to use their puppets when they speak. To aid the discussion, you may wish to use questions like the following:

- Do people always have the same feeling all the time? (No. People have different feelings at different times. Sometimes people are happy. Sometimes people are sad. Sometimes people are scared. Sometimes people are angry.)
- What are some different things people do with their feelings? (Some people may pretend that they don't have any feelings. Other people may try to swallow their feelings down. Still other people may be afraid to show their feelings.)
- Is it bad or wrong to feel angry? (No. Anger is a normal feeling that normal people have twelve to fourteen times a day.)
- How can we can use our anger to work for us? (We can use our anger to play games better, to get us ready to really get going on our homework, or to control ourselves.)
- What are some *harmful* ways to express anger? (When you smack someone or when you don't do your school work.)
- What are some *helpful* ways to express anger? (Take a deep breath, count to ten, ask someone to stop punching; go to your room and tell your toys how angry you feel.)

Even if you choose not to use the above questions, make sure the discussion underscores these concepts.

As the group discusses, use the go-around technique: go around the group, making sure that each child has an opportunity to add to the discussion. You can pass around Della the Dinosaur as the children discuss, giving each child a chance to hold her. Encourage participation, but don't force it. Remember the sixth group rule, which allows a child to pass.

Accept all ideas and answers, explaining or clarifying information where necessary to reinforce learning. Afterward, be sure to thank the children for their participation.

Activity

Have the children take Activity Sheet 2 out of their folders. Point out and read aloud the text on the top of the sheet: "This Person Is Angry." Have the children use their crayons to draw a picture of someone who is angry. Assure the children that they need not make "perfect" drawings—stick figures are fine!

When the children finish, have another go-around. Invite each child to explain his or her drawing to the group. However, don't encourage children to identify the person in their drawings ("my mom" or "my uncle"); the point here is to share ideas, not reveal specific family problems. If a child should make such a revelation, simply comment that Della may know someone she loves very much who might act like the person the child has depicted. Afterward, have the children place their drawings and crayons in their folders.

Basic Facts

Tell the children to take out Basic Facts Worksheet 1. Display copies of Basic Facts Posters 1 and 2. Either read aloud the two basic facts yourself, or have the children read them, one at a time.

1. People in families have many kinds of FEELINGS and all of these feelings are normal.
2. Some ways of showing feelings are HELPFUL; some ways of showing feelings are HARMFUL.

Briefly discuss each fact, checking for understanding. Correct any misconceptions.

Give the children time to complete the bottom half of the worksheet by filling in the blanks. Then have the entire group read the facts aloud. Have the children put their worksheets in their folders along with their Della the Dinosaur puppets.

Wrapping Up

Centering Exercise

Settle the children and then repeat "Breathing Through Your Feet" (page 42).

Affirmation

Involve the group in an affirmation. Stand and join in a circle with the children, holding hands. Go around and have each child share something he or she liked about the group. Start the affirmation yourself: "One thing I liked about the group today was. . . "

Closing

Remain standing in a circle with the children holding hands, and lead the group in the closing activity. You'll use this same activity to end *all* group sessions.

Tell the children that you're going to make a *silent* wish for the child on your right. Then, when you've made the wish, *gently squeeze* the child's hand. The child makes a silent wish for the person on his or her right, then gently squeezes that child's hand, and so on. Continue around the circle until a wish and squeeze come back to you.

Collect the folders. Explain to the group that you will keep the folders and their contents safe until the next group session.

Fill out a copy of the Process and Progress Form (see page 225) or the Progress Notes (see page 226) if you are an experienced leader, as soon as you can after leading the session.

Session 2: Della the Dinosaur Talks About Violence

Objectives

To help the children:

- recognize that people have the choice to use either helpful or harmful ways to express feelings
- learn that it is never okay to choose violence as a way to express feelings of anger
- describe one thing they can do that makes them feel better

Session at a Glance

1. Group Rules: review—2 minutes
2. Centering Exercise: "The Icicle"—3 minutes
3. Feelings Check-in: color Feeling Della—5 minutes
4. Basic Facts Review—3 minutes
5. The Story—7 minutes
6. Discussion—6 minutes
7. Activity: draw a picture of a way you can feel happy (Activity Sheet 3); discuss drawings—8 minutes
8. Basic Facts: (Worksheet 2) read aloud; discuss; fill in blanks; read aloud together—4 minutes
9. Centering Exercise: repeat "The Icicle"—3 minutes
10. Affirmation: share something that you can choose to do that makes you feel happy—3 minutes
11. Closing: have a silent wish and squeeze—1 minute

Preparation

- Display the posterboard copy of the group rules.
- Have the toy Della the Dinosaur and Basic Facts Posters 1 and 2 available.
- Make each child a copy of the Feeling Della (see page 169).
- Staple the children's copies of the Group Rules Contract to the inside back cover of their folders.
- Add the following materials to each folder:
  - a copy of the Feeling Della
  - a copy of Activity Sheet 3 ("This Is What I Do to Feel Happy") and Basic Facts Worksheet 2
- Have each student's folder, pencil, and crayons or markers at his or her place.
- Read through the session plan before meeting.

NOTES

Background and Guidelines

This session stresses—and the session to follow will repeat—that while it is normal and okay to feel angry, it is never okay to express anger in a harmful or violent way. As you discuss the story with the children, you will need to help them see the difference between feeling, thinking, and behaving. The children will need your help to understand that although it's okay for them to feel angry, it's not okay to express their anger through harmful behaviors. The session also foreshadows two helpful ways of dealing with anger: (1) using anger to work for you; (2) expressing anger so you can let it go. Sessions 6 and 7 discuss this differentiation even further. As a leader, you might benefit from looking over the Background and Guidelines sections for those sessions before leading this session.

Remember that even though there may be violence in their homes, the children in your group are going to be loyal to their parents. Be cautious, therefore, not to say negative things about people who choose harmful ways to express anger. Instead, gently but firmly emphasize the choices people have regarding the feeling of anger: (1) to use anger to work for them in a positive way; (2) to express anger in a harmful way; and (3) to express anger in a helpful way. In other words, label the *choice* of using violent behavior to express anger as harmful, without making any negative comment about the person who acts violently.

In this session's basic facts, the children discover that violence is unacceptable behavior ("It is never okay to use violence to express anger"). They learn that people have a choice to use nonviolent and helpful ways to express feelings. Thus, the session helps children begin to understand that they are responsible for how they act on their feelings; it begins to empower the children to take responsibility for their feelings, their thinking, and their actions. Children (and adults) can't control the feelings they get, but they can look at their thinking (their "self-talk") and, if it is negative, change it to positive. They can also do something to make them feel better.

In the story, Della models the concept that children can do good things for themselves—both on their own and with a variety of others—even if they live in a family that uses violence to express anger. Be sure to reinforce this concept: if you feel sad or angry, you can do something that will make you feel better. Understanding this is crucial for building a foundation for the coping strategies that will be described in later sessions.

If you understand that you, too, are responsible for doing what you need to do in order to feel better, and if you have an extensive repertoire of behaviors to help you feel better (engaging in some exercise, listening to music, talking with friends, playing sports, taking a bubble bath, and so on), you'll be more effective as a group leader. So, be ready to share with the children the variety of behaviors and activities *you* use to feel better.

Beginning the Session

Group Rules

Welcome the children and have them sit at their folder. Begin with a quick review of the group's purpose. Remind the youngsters that they all belong to the Della the Dinosaur Group so that they can have fun, learn about chemical dependence, and find out how to feel better and to take better care of themselves. Draw attention to the poster listing the group rules. In a go-around, have the children read the rules one at a time.

1. I will keep what we talk about private.
   We call this confidentiality.
2. I will stay in my seat.
3. I will keep my hands to myself.
4. I will wait for my turn to talk,
   and I will listen carefully when others talk.
5. I won't tease or put other people down.
6. I can "pass" during go-arounds.
7. I will come to every group session.
8. I will make up any class work I miss.

Check for understanding before moving on.

Centering Exercise

Make certain that the children all are comfortable and quiet. Then lead them in the following centering exercise called "The Icicle":

> Close your eyes. Imagine that you are back in a dark and scary place, sort of like outer space. You know that you can get out of that place by breathing through your feet. Well, I'm going to let you in on another secret that will help you get to a safe place. Pay attention, and I'll tell you exactly what to do. The secret is called the Icicle.
>
> Tighten the muscles in your feet and legs really tight; make your feet and legs as stiff as an icicle. (*Pause.*) Now let that cold and stiff icicle melt. Let it melt drip by drip, into a calm and peaceful puddle. Let your legs get loose and very relaxed, and imagine what they would feel like as part of a puddle. (*Pause.*) Tighten your chest, tummy, and trunk area; make it as stiff as an icicle. (*Pause.*) Now let that icicle melt, slowly, drip by

drip, into a puddle. (*Pause.*) Put your arms straight out in front of you, make fists, and pretend that your arms are icicles. (*Pause.*) Now let those icicles melt; let them drip into a puddle, and imagine what they feel like as they drip. (*Pause.*) Tighten the muscles in your shoulders, neck, and head; tighten them into a stiff, cold icicle. Make them very stiff and tight. (*Pause.*) Now let them relax and melt, slowly, very slowly into a puddle. (*Pause.*)

Take every muscle in your whole body; make all those muscles just as stiff and tight as you can. Make your whole self into an icicle. (*Pause.*) Now let yourself melt, from the tip of your toes to the top of your head. Let yourself melt, drip by drip, into a puddle. Let yourself get very loose and relaxed, like smooth water in a puddle. Imagine that your whole body is a calm, quiet, peaceful puddle. (*Pause.*)

You've all just learned another great secret, the Icicle. When you feel scared or frightened, you can let yourself melt—just like an icicle—into a safe, calm, peaceful place.

Feelings Check-in

Do a feelings check-in with the children. Have them take their crayons and Feeling Dellas out of their folders. Direct the children to color in the section on the picture of Della that shows how they're feeling today. For younger children, read the names of the feelings aloud (Angry [red], Scared [purple], Sad [blue], Glad [yellow]). The children can color in more than one feeling, since it's possible to have more than one feeling at a time. Tell the children that if they're having a feeling that is not named on Della, they can add a dinosaur spine to Della in any color they choose.

When the children finish coloring, have a go-around. Begin by sharing your own feelings. Invite each child to say his or her name and to show how he or she is feeling. Be sure to accept each child's feeling(s) and to affirm each child. Afterwards, tell the children that they will be using this same copy of the Feeling Della every time they meet, adding colors at each session. Therefore, make certain the children put the sheet away safely in their folders.

Basic Facts Review

To help the children review their last session and the basic facts learned so far, show them Basic Facts Posters 1 and 2:

1. People in families have many kinds of FEELINGS, and all of these feelings are normal.
2. Some ways of showing feelings are HELPFUL; some ways of showing feelings are HARMFUL.

In a go-around, ask a child to read the first fact aloud and to explain what it means. If a youngster has trouble, don't contradict or judge, simply clarify the explanation. Then ask all the children to repeat the fact together. Repeat the process for each fact.

Exploring the Story

The Story

Have the children get comfortable for today's story. Be sure to use the toy Della and allow *her* to tell the following:

> Hello, girls and boys! It's so good to see you again. When we met last time, we talked about anger. Do you remember? Anger is a normal feeling. In fact, we said that people and dinosaurs usually feel angry about twelve to fourteen times a day. So, you see, it's okay to feel angry.
>
> Today, I'd like to talk to you about ways to *cope* with your anger. Coping means handling a problem you can't change or solve. There are three ways to cope with anger. The first way is to use your anger to work for you. A second way is to express anger in a harmful way. The third way is to express your anger in a helpful way so you can let it go. It's good for people and dinosaurs to use their anger to work for them. It's good for people and dinosaurs to express their anger in helpful ways so they can let it go. But, some people and dinosaurs haven't learned how to express their anger in helpful ways. They express it in harmful ways.
>
> They express their anger by yelling or blaming others. They break things. Or they push, shove, kick, slap, hit, or punch others. Sometimes people express their anger even by killing. They may wreck their house or hurt their pets. They may even hurt the people they love and live with. If you wonder why people act this way, it's because they don't choose to learn more helpful ways to express their anger. Instead, people who act like this are using violent ways to express their anger.
>
> Maybe you think that only bad people or criminals use violent ways to express their anger. But that's not true. Lots of different people use violent ways to express their anger. These people could have any kind of job. They could be doctors, lawyers, teachers, or fire fighters. They could be police officers, janitors, truck drivers, nurses, or secretaries. They could be moms or dads, aunts or uncles, grandmas or grandpas, even sisters or brothers. They could be friends, neighbors, or baby-sitters. And they could be adults or children.
>
> Sometimes these same people may choose more helpful ways to express their anger so they can let it go. They may talk to someone about their feeling of anger. They may take time out, write in a journal, draw a picture, exercise, or count to ten. They may hammer nails in a piece of scrap wood or punch a punching bag or a pillow. All these ways of expressing anger help people let go of their angry feelings.

Like most children, I have all the usual feelings, even though I'm a dinosaur. Sometimes I feel happy. Sometimes I feel sad. Sometimes I feel scared. Sometimes I feel angry. Some days I wake up in a sad or angry mood, but I don't have to stay that way. I can do things that will make me feel happy.

Here are some things I can choose to do that make me feel happy:

1. I can play dinosaur tennis.
2. I can paint a picture in my mind, pretending that I'm riding the Loch Ness Monster.
3. I can play "Elimination" with Megan and Joanna, the Stegosaurus twins.
4. I can call my grandma and tell her a joke.
5. I can play video games with my brother.
6. I can ride my dinosaur bike.
7. I can read my favorite book, *Encyclopedia Brown*.
8. I can watch "Mr. Wizard," my favorite science TV show.

Maybe you can make a list of things you can choose to do to make you feel happy.

Well, I'd better go. See you soon!

Discussion

Lead a discussion to help group members better understand the facts—the key concepts—presented in the story. Let the children use their puppets when they speak, and let them hold Della the Dinosaur as they share. As the group discusses, remember to go around, making sure that each child has an opportunity to add to the discussion. Encourage participation, but don't force it. Remember the group rule that allows a child to pass. Accept all ideas and answers, explaining or clarifying information where necessary to reinforce learning. To aid the discussion, you may use questions like the following:

- What are three ways to cope with anger? (You can (1) use your anger to work for you; (2) express your anger in a harmful way; (3) express your anger in a helpful way so you can let it go.)
- What are some helpful ways to express anger so you can let it go? (You may talk to someone about your feeling of anger, take time out, write in a journal, draw a picture, exercise, count to ten, hammer nails in a piece of scrap wood, or punch a punching bag or a pillow.)
- What are some violent ways to express anger? (Yell at or blame others, break things, push, shove, kick, slap, hit, punch, or even kill.)

- Are criminals the only people who use violent ways to express their anger? (No. Just about anyone, including friends and relatives, could choose to use violent ways to express anger.)
- If Della wakes up feeling sad or angry, does she have to stay feeling that way all day? (No. She can choose to do something that will make her feel better.)
- What are some things Della could choose to do in order to feel happy? (Look for answers that reflect the children's understanding of the list Della shared in today's story.)

Even if you choose not to use the above questions, make sure the discussion underscores these concepts.

Activity

Ask the children to retrieve their copies of Activity Sheet 3. Read aloud the title at the top of the sheet: "This Is What I Do to Feel Happy." Ask the children to use their crayons to draw a picture of something they can choose to do that makes them feel happy. Remember, if a child refuses to draw, allow him or her to write.

When the children finish, have another go-around. Invite each child to explain his or her drawing to the group. Afterward, have the children put their drawings and crayons in their folders.

Basic Facts

Tell the children to take out Basic Facts Worksheet 2. Either read aloud the new basics facts yourself, or have the children read them, one at a time.

3. Some people choose to use VIOLENT ways to express their anger. They may yell, blame, throw, break, push, shove, kick, slap, hit, punch, or kill.
4. It is NEVER okay to use violent ways to express ANGER.
5. People can choose to learn NONVIOLENT and HELPFUL ways to express their anger.

Briefly discuss each fact, checking for understanding. Correct any misconceptions.

Give the children time to complete the bottom half of the worksheet by filling in the blanks. Then have the group read the facts aloud. Have the children put their worksheets in their folders along with their Della the Dinosaur puppets.

Wrapping Up

Centering Exercise

Settle the children and then repeat "The Icicle" (page 51).

Affirmation

Involve the group in an affirmation. Stand and join in a circle with the children, holding hands. Go around and have the children share something that they can choose to do that makes them feel happy. Start the affirmation yourself: "One thing I can choose to do to feel happy is. . . "

Closing

Remain standing in a circle with the children, holding hands, and lead the group in the closing activity. Tell the children that you're going to make a *silent* wish for the child on your right. Then, when you've made the wish, *gently squeeze* the child's hand. The child makes a silent wish for the person on his or her right, then gently squeezes that child's hand, and so on. Continue around the circle until a wish and squeeze come back to you.

Collect the folders. Explain to the group that you will keep the folders and their contents safe until the next group session.

Fill out a copy of the Process and Progress Form (see page 225) or the Progress Notes (see page 226), if you are an experienced leader, as soon as you can after leading the session.

Session 3: Della the Dinosaur Talks About Violence in Her Family

Objectives

To help the children:

- identify ways children might behave if their family uses violence to express feelings
- recognize that parents usually love their children, even if they use violence to express anger
- understand that although children may feel hate for parents who use violence, children still usually love them

Session at a Glance

1. Group Rules: review—2 minutes
2. Centering Exercise: "A Safe, Warm Place"—3 minutes
3. Feelings Check-in: color Feeling Della—5 minutes
4. Basic Facts Review—4 minutes
5. The Story—7 minutes
6. Discussion—6 minutes
7. Activity: draw a feeling picture of your family (Activity Sheet 4); discuss drawings—8 minutes
8. Basic Facts: (Worksheet 3) read aloud; discuss; fill in blanks; read aloud together—3 minutes
9. Centering Exercise: repeat "A Safe, Warm Place"—3 minutes
10. Affirmation: share something that you liked about today's story—3 minutes
11. Closing: have a silent wish and squeeze—1 minute

Preparation

- Display the posterboard copy of the group rules.
- Have the toy Della the Dinosaur and Basic Facts Posters 1-5 available.
- Add the following materials to each folder:

  - a copy of Activity Sheet 4 ("A Feeling Picture of My Family")

  - a copy of Basic Facts Worksheet 3
- Have each student's folder, pencil, crayons or markers at his or her place.
- Read through the session plan before meeting.

NOTES

Background and Guidelines

People who use violence to express feelings usually begin to use violence in small and infrequent episodes, which then escalate into more severe and frequent episodes. As the violent pattern develops, it becomes more habitual.

Like people who are chemically dependent, people who use violence have a strong defense system. Their defenses include: denial ("I didn't hurt you"); projection or blaming ("You deserve to be hit. Look at what you did!"); minimizing ("I didn't get angry. I just raised my voice"); rationalizing ("So what if I lose my temper. At least I always stay home"). Violent people also use lies and excuses to defend their behavior.

Of these defenses, projection and rationalizing seem to be the most commonly used by people who choose to use violence. Typically, their spouses and children soon tend to believe the defenses. In fact, they may even believe that the violent behavior is their fault, that their "provocative" behavior or mistakes actually *cause* the violence. Believing that they've caused the violence, many spouses and children go on to believe that they can *change* or *control* it. Thus, they respond to the violent behavior by changing their own behavior. They may cease to express their own needs and desires or their own anger for fear it will cause a violent episode. They may assume responsibility for the feelings of the person who chooses to use violence. Finally, they may start taking over the violent person's chores.

Spouses may begin to feel hopeless or powerless. They may see themselves as victims and as failures and as being unable to help themselves. The plight of such spouses is similar to that of a satellite revolving around a planet, stuck in its gravitational pull. Like hapless satellites, many spouses of violent persons are unable to break away, act independently, steer their own course.

If spouses could break away from the pull of the violent person, they would stop feeling responsible for the person's violent behavior and would stop trying to control it. Instead, they would begin to deal with their own feelings, would begin to set limits on inappropriate behavior, and begin to set goals for themselves.

Spouses aren't the only family members who alter their behavior in response to a family member's violent behavior. Because children from families that use violence to express feelings may suffer from traumatic shock and experience universal feelings of fear, anger, sadness, anxiety, loneliness, and hopelessness, they change their behaviors and often assume the familial "survival" roles described in literature about children of chemically dependent people. Children take on these roles to survive in the violent home and to make life there less painful. The roles typically described for children in a dysfunctional family are *superhero, lost child, scapegoat,* and *mascot.*

Superheroes (or "over-acheivers" or "too-good-to-be-true" children) generally—and mistakenly—believe that if they are only good enough, or perfect enough, their family's problems will be solved. These children try to help out at home, get good grades, be therapists to their parents. They do anything and everything they can to help parents solve their problems. These children live in the misconception that their behavior (if it's good enough) can control or cure negative parental behavior. Superhero children generally end up feeling like failures, because no matter how good they are, their "perfect" behavior can never be good enough to make their parents stop fighting, using violence, or hurting others. Living in the misconception that if they are only "perfect" enough they can change parental behavior, superheroes may become very rigid and perfectionist. They may overreact and become unduly upset over the slightest criticism from an authority figure, such as a teacher, coach, or clergyperson.

Superheroes are outwardly successful; the family can point to them, feel proud, and say, "We're okay." Superheroes pay a price, however. Generally, they experience feelings of hurt, inadequacy, confusion, guilt, fear, and low self- esteem. They seem to be able to do anything, *except* what they want most to do—make their family well.

Lost children may feel personally responsible for the parental chaos in a violent home. Rather than trying to control that chaos, however, lost children try becoming invisible. If invisible, they won't be held accountable for parental stress or upset. These children might spend a lot of time by themselves, away from other family members, "lost" in their own worlds. They may become overeaters or underachievers in school, or they may become isolated and withdrawn, seeing themselves as alone, helpless, vulnerable, and powerless. Lost children give a family with violence some relief. Pointing to the quiet, lost child, a family can think that everything's all right in the family. On the inside, lost children feel unimportant, lonely, hurt, abandoned, fearful, and defeated.

Scapegoats tend to be the lightning rods for anger in a family. These children may act out their own anger by fighting or yelling at home or at school. They tend to get themselves in trouble and, in this way, focus attention away from the spouse by drawing the anger of the violent parent to themselves in a self-sacrificing rescue attempt. Scapegoats feel hurt and abandoned, angry and rejected, and totally inadequate; they possess little or no self-esteem.

Mascots tend to provide comic relief for the family by acting as family clowns. Like scapegoats, they focus attention away from the problem of the violent parent, or deflect that violence through humor. These children generally see themselves as "jokes." Thus, they have low self-esteem and feel frightened, lonely, anxious, inadequate, and unimportant. Mascots may be diagnosed as having an Attention-Deficit Hyperactivity Disorder, or they may have learning disabilities in school.

These survival roles aren't meant to be labels or rigid categories. In fact, children in violent families may exhibit characteristics of several different roles at the same time; or, over time, they may adopt different roles. For instance, a younger child who acts as a scapegoat may become a superhero after an older sibling (who has played the role) leaves home. Likewise, children from violent families may exhibit other traits that don't necessarily fit the roles identified here. These roles are stressed to alert you to behaviors *typically* found in violent homes, behaviors you might find in the members of your group.

Being familiar with these roles, you can help the children deal with their *ambivalence* toward their parents. Often, children from violent homes have intense feelings of both love and hatred toward their parents, often accompanied by feelings of guilt due to their hatred. Remember to accept both the positive and the negative feelings the children may express about their parents. Help the children recognize that having such opposite feelings at the same time is confusing, but normal.

In this session's story, the children will see how Della feels and behaves ambivalently—she loves her dad, but hates how he uses violence; she thinks he is neat, but is afraid of him. In the face of parental violence, Della may experience intense fear, sadness, anxiety, loneliness, guilt, hopelessness, and so on. The intensity of these feelings may also increase at one time and diminish at another. The behavior of Della's parents also varies: sometimes they are loving; sometimes they fight and yell. As the children encounter this variance in today's story and discussion, help them to see that it's normal and okay for people to have different feelings at different times, but that violent behavior is not normal or okay. Also, remind the children that in some families *moms*, not dads, use violence to express anger.

During the activity, when the children share "feeling pictures" of their families, it's a good idea to point out that feelings are transitory and of different intensities. Like clouds in the sky, feelings come and go and may come back, and feelings may be stormy or mild. This foreshadows what the children will learn about feelings later on (in Session 5) and helps them begin to recognize that they can learn to handle the intense feelings they experience as a result of living in a family that uses violence to express anger.

Finally, as you lead the children through this session, be alert for a rise in their anxiety levels. Della's story presents the effects of family violence on families and children in a nonthreatening way. Still, because the story is likely to touch "close to home," expect the children to react. Be ready to validate and tolerate both their feelings and their anxiety. This will lay the groundwork for the children to recognize and accept their feelings on their own.

Beginning the Session

Group Rules

Welcome the children and begin with a quick review of the group rules. Draw attention to the poster listing the group rules. In a go-around, have the children read the rules one at a time.

1. I will keep what we talk about private.
   We call this confidentiality.
2. I will stay in my seat.
3. I will keep my hands to myself.
4. I will wait for my turn to talk,
   and I will listen carefully when others talk.
5. I won't tease or put other people down.
6. I can "pass" during go-arounds.
7. I will come to every group session.
8. I will make up any class work I miss.

Check for understanding before moving on.

Centering Exercise

Lead the group in the following centering exercise called "A Safe, Warm Place."

> Close your eyes. You're back in a dark, cold, and scary place, like an abandoned mine. I'm going to tell you another secret to get you to a warm, safe place. I'm going to tell you how to paint a picture in your mind.
>
> Imagine or pretend that you're in a place that you like a lot. It's a place where you feel very relaxed and comfortable. This place may be different for each person. It may be a bedroom. It may be a special corner in your house. It may be a secret place in your attic. It may be a place outside that's very beautiful. No matter where it is for you, it's a place where you feel very safe and warm and cozy.
>
> Pretend that you're there right now and that those safe and warm and cozy feelings are all around you. You're feeling very relaxed, very warm, very safe, and very cozy and comfortable. When you come back to where you are now, you'll feel very good and ready to work hard.

Feelings Check-in

Do a feelings check-in with the children. Have them take their crayons and Feeling Dellas out of their folders. Direct the children to color in the section on Della that shows how they're feeling today. For younger children, read the names of the feelings aloud (Angry [red], Scared [purple], Sad [blue], Glad [yellow]). The children can color in more than one feeling, since it's possible to have more than one feeling at a time. Tell the children that if they're having a feeling that is not named, they can add a dinosaur spine to Della in any color they choose. Also point out that if they need to, the children can re-color a space.

When the children finish coloring, have a go-around, beginning by sharing your own feelings. Invite each child to say his or her name and to show how he or she is feeling. Be sure to accept each child's feeling(s) and to affirm each child. Ask the children to return the Feeling Dellas to their folders.

Basic Facts Review

To help the children review the basic facts learned so far, show them Basic Facts Posters 1-5:

1. People in families have many kinds of FEELINGS, and all of these feelings are normal.
2. Some ways of showing feelings are HELPFUL; some ways of showing feelings are HARMFUL.
3. Some people choose to use VIOLENT ways to express their anger. They may yell, blame, throw, break, push, shove, kick, slap, hit, punch, or kill.
4. It is NEVER okay to use violent ways to express ANGER.
5. People can choose to learn NONVIOLENT and HELPFUL ways to express their anger.

In a go-around, ask a child to read the first fact aloud and to explain what it means. If a youngster has trouble, don't contradict or judge, simply clarify the explanation. Then ask all the children to repeat the fact together. Repeat the process for each fact.

Exploring the Story

The Story

Have the children get comfortable to hear today's story. Be sure to use the toy Della and allow *her* to tell the following:

> I'd like to tell you what it's like to live in a family where someone chooses violence to express anger. I'd like to tell you about *my* family.
>
> My dad's name is Brad Brontosaurus. I love him a lot. Sometimes he plays dinosaur tennis with me. We hit the ball with our tails. Sometimes he reads me stories. He tucks me in at night. Sometimes, my dad takes our whole family swimming at Wild Water Wonderland.
>
> My mom's name is Becky Brontosaurus. I love her a lot. She takes me shopping for toys and clothes at Dinosaurs R Us. Sometimes she takes me to Bush Gardens. We ride the Loch Ness Monster. I have a great time with my mom.
>
> My brother's name is Danny the Dinosaur. He's a little squirt, but he thinks he's some sort of Junior Ninja or something. He's always practicing his karate kicks on me. Sometimes those kicks hurt! But, I guess I like Danny. I like him best when we pretend we are the "Dinosaur Detectives," and we solve big mysteries just like Encyclopedia Brown.
>
> Well, anyway, like I said, I love my dad and mom. But sometimes they fight, and when they do, it scares me a lot. Sometimes they get angry at each other. They yell at each other. Sometimes they yell at Danny and me, too. Once, Dad got so angry that he pushed Mom up against the wall. Mom cried. Another time, Dad got so angry that he slapped Mom's face. He tried to choke her. Mom started screaming for help. Danny and I tried to get Dad to let go of Mom. He finally let go of her. But then he got really angry at Danny and me. I was really scared!
>
> Sometimes when my parents fight, Mom says she's going to call the police. Once she said that she was going to leave Dad.
>
> Sometimes my dad is really calm and very nice. But other times he gets really angry. Then he's just like a volcano that's exploding. I'm afraid of Dad when he's violent. I'm afraid he's going to hurt someone—maybe my mom, maybe Danny, or maybe even me. Even when Dad's not violent, I worry about when he might explode again. It's hard for little dinosaurs to know where and when it's safe.
>
> If you think that I sound confused, you're right. You see, sometimes my parents get along well together. They act like they love each other and me and Danny. But other times, they fight. Dad gets violent. Then I'm scared that they don't love each other, or Danny and me. After my parents fight, they stay feeling angry. Then they might

ignore me or yell at me. They might hit me or send me to my room. I'm never sure what I've done to make them so angry.

When I see other dinosaurs at the park, I think to myself, "Boy, there's a happy dinosaur family." I wonder why my family can't be like theirs.

Sometimes my parents are fighting when I have to go to school. Then, when I go to school, I think about the way my dad hurts my mom. I think about that a lot. I worry that Mom might leave Dad. I worry about what will happen to me and Danny. I get real scared, real sad, and sometimes real angry. Sometimes, I just stay home from school. I want to make sure that no one gets hurt.

I used to wonder what "feeling color" each person in my family would be. I would color my dad yellow and *very* red, because sometimes he's nice, and sometimes he's angry. I would color my mom blue, because she seems so sad a lot of the time. I would color Danny red, because he's angry a lot. I would color myself purple and blue, because I'm scared and sad all at the same time. I wonder what a feeling picture of your family would look like.

The next time we meet, I want to tell you about this real neat lady I met. She helped me with my feelings. But for now, I gotta go. I'll see you again soon.

Discussion

Lead a discussion to help group members better understand the facts—the key concepts—presented in the story. Help the children identify the variety of behaviors Della's family exhibited in the story. For instance: Dad is nice sometimes and violent at other times; Mom says she will leave Dad, but doesn't; Della and Danny worry and try to get their parents to stop fighting; Della worries and stays home from school.

As the group discusses, remember to use the go-around technique, making sure that each child has an opportunity to add to the discussion. Encourage participation, but don't force it. Remember the group rule that allows a child to pass. Accept all ideas and answers, explaining or clarifying information where necessary to reinforce learning and to correct misconceptions. To aid the discussion, you may wish to use questions like the following:

- How does Della's dad, Brad, act toward others in his family? (Sometimes he's nice: plays tennis with Della; reads to her; tucks her in at night. Sometimes he's angry: yells at Della's mom; pushes, slaps, and once even choked her; gets angry at Della and Danny.)
- How does Della's mom, Becky, act toward others in her family? (Sometimes she's nice: takes Della shopping; rides the Loch Ness Monster with Della. Sometimes she fights with Della's dad; says she's going to call the police; threatens to leave, but doesn't.)
- What are some things that Danny, Della's little brother, does? (He practices his karate kicks on Della. He also plays Dinosaur Detectives with Della.)

- Does Della know what makes her parents fight? (No. Sometimes her dad is nice, but sometimes he's very angry. Della never knows how he will feel or act.)
- What are some feelings Della has about her parents? (Della worries a lot. She gets confused. She loves her parents, but feels scared, sad, and angry.)
- What are some of Della's worries? (She worries that someone in her family will get hurt. She worries that her mom will leave her dad. She worries about what will happen to Danny and her.)

Even if you choose not to use the above questions, make sure the discussion underscores these concepts.

Activity

Ask the children to retrieve their copies of Activity Sheet 4. Have the children use their crayons to draw a picture that shows all their family members. Tell them to color each member with the color that shows the feeling he or she has most often. Remind them of the colors Della used to draw her family. Again, assure the children that they need not make "perfect" drawings. However, they should color each person with the appropriate feeling color. If a child refuses to draw, give him or her the option to write.

When the children finish, have another go-around. Invite each child to explain his or her drawing to the group. Afterward, have the children put their drawings and crayons in their folders.

Basic Facts

Tell the children to take out Basic Facts Worksheet 3. Either read aloud the new basic facts yourself, or ask different children to read them, one at a time.

6. Parents usually LOVE their children, even when parents are choosing to use violent ways to express their anger.
7. Children usually LOVE their parents, although they may feel HATE for the parents if the parents are using violent ways to express their anger.

Briefly discuss each fact, checking for understanding. Correct any misconceptions.

Give the children time to complete the bottom half of the worksheet by filling in the blanks. Then have the group read the facts aloud. Have the children put their worksheets in their folders along with their Della the Dinosaur puppets.

Wrapping Up

Centering Exercise

Settle the children and then repeat "A Safe, Warm Place" (page 63).

Affirmation

Involve the group in an affirmation. Stand and join in a circle with the children, holding hands. Go around and have the children share something that they especially liked about today's story. Start the affirmation yourself: "One thing I liked about today's story . . . "

Closing

Remain standing in a circle with the children, holding hands, and lead the group in the closing activity. Tell the children that you're going to make a silent wish for the child on your right. Then, when you've made the wish, gently squeeze the child's hand. The child makes a silent wish for the person on his or her right, then gently squeezes that child's hand, and so on. Continue around the circle until a wish and squeeze come back to you.

Collect the folders. Explain to the group that you will keep the folders and their contents safe until the next group session.

Fill out a copy of the Process and Progress Form (see page 225) or the Progress Notes (see page 226), if you are an experienced leader, as soon as you can after leading the session.

Session 4: Della the Dinosaur Meets Mrs. Owl

Objectives

- learn that children don't cause and can't control or change a parent's use of violence to express anger
- discover four things children in violent families can do to take care of themselves

Session at a Glance

1. Group Rules: review—1 minute
2. Centering Exercise: "The Meadow"—3 minutes
3. Feelings Check-in: color Feeling Della—5 minutes
4. Basic Facts Review—5 minutes
5. The Story—8 minutes
6. Discussion—6 minutes
7. Activity: make a Mrs. Owl puppet (Activity Sheet 5)—7 minutes
8. Basic Facts: (Worksheet 4) read aloud; discuss; fill in blanks; read aloud together—3 minutes
9. Centering Exercise: repeat "The Meadow"—3 minutes
10. Affirmation: share one fact you will remember from today's session—3 minutes
11. Closing: have a silent wish and squeeze—1 minute

Preparation

- Display the posterboard copy of the group rules.
- Find an appealing, cuddly, stuffed toy owl to portray Mrs. Owl. Look for a friendly-looking owl, and add eyeglasses and an inexpensive, imitation pearl necklace.
- Have the toy Della the Dinosaur and Basic Facts Posters 1-7 available.
- Have tape or glue sticks available for today's activity.
- To save time during the session—especially if group members are kindergartners or first graders—precut the Mrs. Owl puppets (body, beak, and wings) from the copies of Activity Sheet 5. This gives the children more time to color and decorate their work. Make a sample puppet for the children to use as a model.
- Add the following materials to each folder:

  - a copy of Activity Sheet 5 ("Mrs. Owl Puppet")

  - a copy of Basic Facts Worksheet 4
- Have each student's folder, pencil, and crayons or markers at his or her place.
- Make a poster listing the following violent ways people might use to express anger:

- yelling	- kicking
- blaming others	- slapping
- breaking things	- hitting
- pushing	- punching
- shoving	- killing

Use the poster during this session's story.

- Copy the three Cs (from #8 on Basic Facts Worksheet 4) onto a piece of posterboard or newsprint to display during the session. (Note: If you plan to involve the children in the optional Session 10, save this poster for use in that session.)
- Read through the session plan before meeting.

NOTES

Background and Guidelines

Because children don't possess the knowledge and perspective necessary to correctly identify the stresses in their family, they often try to create order out of the chaos that they do see. However, given their developmental levels, they generally do so in "childish," egocentric, and incorrect ways. They develop misconceptions typical of children living in at-risk families. For example, children often believe that their family's problems are their fault, that they've *caused* a parent's violence: "My mom and dad fight because I talk back too much." Or, some children try to *control* parental violence by trying to intervene and stop the parents from fighting. The usual result is that the parent becomes angry with the children and may become abusive with them. Children may also try to control the parents by telling them to stop fighting or to seek professional help. Unfortunately, although children may believe that they have the power necessary to insist that a parent get help, they don't have such power. Thus, when children are unsuccessful in their controlling efforts, they feel like failures and suffer from low self-esteem.

When children believe that they've caused a parent's violence, they often think that they can *change* it as well. Children try to effect change through a variety of means: by getting good grades in school, by doing all the chores around the home, or by finding another way to bring honor to the family (through their efforts in sports, dance, art, and so on). Again, these efforts won't be effective, and again the children will feel like failures.

Della feels this way. But in this session, she meets a caring professional, Mrs. Owl, who assures her that what she says will be held in confidence, and so Della begins to trust and talk. Della's opening of her "wound" is the beginning of getting better. She feels uncomfortable talking about parental violence, but as she talks and as Mrs. Owl normalizes her feelings, Della begins the process of accepting her situation and learning to cope with her feelings.

Along with Della, the children meet Mrs. Owl, who corrects their misconceptions by teaching them the three Cs: children (1) don't *c*ause, (2) can't *c*ontrol, and (3) can't *c*hange a parent's use of violence. This will be new information for many of the children, and they may resist it. While respecting the children's feelings and opinions, you should be ready to help them understand that they really don't have the power to cause, control, or change parental behavior. Acknowledge to the children that it would be wonderful if children could control or change another person's behavior. Unfortunately, children don't have that kind of power. Point out that not even a spouse of a violent person has such power. Help the children see that people who use violence to express anger will change their behavior only when they realize how severe the consequences of such behavior are and decide that they want to change.

It is hoped that by the time the children complete the eleven sessions of this group, they will be able to abandon their efforts to control or change a violent parent. The three Cs start this *detachment* process. Only after children give up the belief that they are responsible for the family's problems can they focus on taking care of themselves (self-preservation) in a positive and healthy way.

As group leader, it's important that you understand that detachment is difficult for children from violent homes, because they often have great difficulties with *enmeshment* and *boundaries.* Enmeshment is an aspect of co-dependent behavior that refers to people's inability to set boundaries between themselves and others. Enmeshed children from violent homes often take on parental feelings ("If Mom is sad, I must be sad, too") or feel responsible for fixing parental problems ("I have to do something to stop Mom and Dad from fighting and make them feel better"). Enmeshed children often fail to develop separate identities.

Boundaries are important because part of normal, healthy development is to separate and individuate from the caretaker and to develop a sense of personal integrity and internal resources in order to form relationships and to deal with the stresses of life. It's healthy for children (indeed, for everyone) to develop a sense of separateness from the loved one, a sense of individuality that allows for closeness when needed. Finally, it's also healthy to develop a sense of personal space and integrity that allows children to set limits when they don't desire closeness.

As in Session 3, watch for feelings of ambivalence to surface in the children. Most children from violent homes have trouble distinguishing between a person and a person's behavior. As leader, identify and validate both the positive and the negative feelings the children may express. Today's story explains that children may love a person but hate the person's behavior at the same time. Make sure that the children understand that feeling like this is normal, and that you understand that it is also very confusing.

By teaching the children the three Cs, the session also aims at helping the children deal with the factors of *co-dependence*, *detachment*, and *empowerment.* It's important that you understand how each of these factors affects the children.

Although the term "co-dependence" is not introduced to the children, the group is designed to help them learn alternatives to co-dependent behavior. A person's behavior may be described as *co-dependent* when (1) a person feels responsible for another's feelings, problems, or behavior; or (2) a person doesn't take action on his or her own behalf, but simply reacts to the behaviors or feelings of another. Co-dependent people may be very controlling of another, or they may worry so much about another that they don't pay attention to themselves, thus never fulfilling their own potential.

In Session 2, the children discovered that they can do some things to take care of themselves. Knowing this is the first step to learning alternatives to co-dependent behavior. As the group progresses, the children will learn that they don't have to depend on someone else for their feelings, but can be responsible for themselves, can learn how to deal effectively with feelings, and can choose to do things that they enjoy.

As mentioned above, learning the three Cs also helps the children begin the *detachment* process. This doesn't mean that children cut themselves off from their parents, but that they give up believing that they are responsible for a parent's problem. Children discover that they can love and care for a parent and can express that love and concern without having to control a parent or fix a parent's problem. Finally, the three Cs *empower* the children. They help the children begin to turn their focus away from their family's problems and to turn it on themselves in positive and healthy ways. The session also introduces four steps the children can take to empower themselves. Children from homes where violence is used to express anger can:

1. Find a SAFE place for themselves.
2. Ask a grown-up for HELP if the parents are out of control with their violence.
3. Learn to RECOGNIZE, ACCEPT, and SHARE their feelings.
4. Choose to learn NONVIOLENT ways to express their own feelings.

Spend time helping the children commit these empowering steps to memory.

Since many children think that such empowerment is a form of selfishness, be ready to help them see the difference between selfishness and self-preservation. For example, you might ask a child to imagine that he or she is one of three people on an island, with only one piece of cake to eat. Eating the whole piece is selfishness; giving it to the other two people and having none yourself is being a martyr; dividing the cake into three pieces and claiming your share is self-preservation.

The children need to realize that self-preservation is a positive activity and means taking care of themselves in age-appropriate ways. The children can't do this if they're engaged in the futile and overwhelming task of trying to fix their parents' problems.

Finally, make sure the children clearly get the message that they should *not* try to protect a parent from the violence of another parent. Realize, however, that most of the children will not like this message. They will want to intervene—"Do you think I'm just going to sit there and watch him beat on Mom?" Gently acknowledge that many children feel this way, but go on to explain that children can't protect parents. Strongly encourage the children to keep themselves safe and to ask another grown-up for help. It may be only after the children hear the facts in this session that they will begin to recognize the futility of trying to control parental violence.

Throughout the session, use your knowledge of the group members' individual situations to tailor the story and discussion to speak to those situations. If, for example, you find that the children refuse to let go of the belief that they cause the violence in their homes, spend more time discussing that issue. In fact, if you feel that the children's needs dictate it, use two meeting times to present this session. For the sake of the children, this session's concepts and ideas deserve whatever time it takes to help the children understand them. Also, remember that it takes time for children to change their belief system.

Beginning the Session

Group Rules

Welcome the children. Begin with a quick review of the group's rules. Draw attention to the poster listing the group rules. In a go-around, have the children read the rules one at a time.

1. I will keep what we talk about private.
   We call this confidentiality.
2. I will stay in my seat.
3. I will keep my hands to myself.
4. I will wait for my turn to talk,
   and I will listen carefully when others talk.
5. I won't tease or put other people down.
6. I can "pass" during go-arounds.
7. I will come to every group session.
8. I will make up any class work I miss.

Check for understanding before moving on.

Centering Exercise

Lead the group in the following centering exercise called "The Meadow."

> Imagine that it's the month of April. You're in a meadow with soft green grass. The meadow is surrounded by beautiful dogwood trees—so full that the blossoms look like a snowfall. You can smell the fresh scent of spring in the air. The sky above is bright blue and dotted with puffy clouds. You are there with a very good friend—somebody you really trust, like a mom or dad, a best friend, or maybe someone you were once close to, a pet, or even a favorite stuffed toy animal. You feel very safe and secure with this friend.

You begin to experience a difficult feeling—anger or sadness or even fear. Your friend helps you with your feeling. Your friend tells you that even though you have this feeling, you are safe. You tell your friend how angry, sad, or scared you feel. As you talk to your friend, you feel the feeling in your body, in whatever form it takes for you. Your friend is there to keep you safe while you feel it and describe it. You may beat your fists against the ground, or cry, or even shake. Whatever you do, it's okay, because your friend is completely trustworthy.

After you've finished telling your friend about the feeling, experienced it in your body, and maybe even pounded, cried, or shook, you begin to feel better. You experience a sense of release, a calmness and peacefulness you haven't felt for a long time. You begin to be aware of the meadow again. It's as if you're seeing the dogwoods, the sky, and the clouds for the first time. You feel a sense of thanks and appreciation for the beauty of the surroundings, and you again feel in control, calm, and peaceful.

Feelings Check-in

Do a feelings check-in with the children. Have them take their crayons and Feeling Dellas out of their folders. Direct the children to color in the section on Della that shows how they're feeling today. For younger children, read the names of the feelings aloud (Angry [red], Scared [purple], Sad [blue], Glad [yellow]). The children can color in more than one feeling, since it's possible to have more than one feeling at a time. Tell the children that if they're having a feeling that is not named, they can add a dinosaur spine to Della in any color they choose. Also point out that if they need to, the children can re-color a space.

When the children finish coloring, have a go-around, beginning by sharing your own feelings. Invite each child to say his or her name and to show how he or she is feeling. Be sure to accept each child's feeling(s) and to affirm each child. Ask the children to return the Feeling Dellas to their folders.

Basic Facts Review

To help the children review the basic facts learned so far, show them Basic Facts Posters 1-7:

1. People in families have many kinds of FEELINGS, and all of these feelings are normal.
2. Some ways of showing feelings are HELPFUL; some ways of showing feelings are HARMFUL.
3. Some people choose to use VIOLENT ways to express their anger. They may yell, blame, throw, break, push, shove, kick, slap, hit, punch, or kill.
4. It is NEVER okay to use violent ways to express ANGER.

5. People can choose to learn NONVIOLENT and HELPFUL ways to express their anger.
6. Parents usually LOVE their children, even when parents are choosing to use violent ways to express their anger.
7. Children usually LOVE their parents, although they may feel HATE for the parents if the parents are using violent ways to express their anger.

In a go-around, ask a child to read the first fact aloud and to explain what it means. If a youngster has trouble, don't contradict or judge, simply clarify the explanation. Then ask all the children to repeat the fact together. Repeat the process for each fact.

Exploring the Story

The Story

If you were able to get a toy owl, have it—or a Mrs. Owl puppet, made from Activity Sheet 5—ready to introduce to the children during the story to portray Mrs. Owl. Have the children get comfortable to hear today's story. Be sure to use the toy Della and allow *her* to tell the following:

> Usually I like school. I like my friends and my teacher. I especially like science. I think it's cool. But like I told you last time, I used to worry about my mom and dad fighting. I started staying home and missing a lot of school. One day, my teacher said to me, "I'm worried about you, Della. You've missed a lot of school lately, and it's hurting your grades. You seem to be feeling worried lately, but maybe you don't understand why you're feeling that way. I think you should meet Mrs. Owl. She's someone who comes to our school. She talks with children like you about the way they feel."
>
> *(Take a moment to introduce the toy Mrs. Owl or the Mrs. Owl puppet to the children. Then go on with the story.)*
>
> Well, I met Mrs. Owl. At first, she asked me some easy questions like what was my favorite food, where I lived, and what I wanted to be when I grew up. Then she asked a hard question. She asked me about the stresses in my life. Mrs. Owl explained that *stress* is anything that makes me feel worried or upset.
>
> I knew that I was worried about my parents' fighting. I was worried whether Mom, Danny, or I would get hurt. I was worried that Mom would call the police, then maybe Dad would have to go to jail. I worried that Mom might leave, and then what would happen to me and Danny? I was also worried that when Mom and Dad fought it was my fault. You know, like maybe I'd done something wrong.
>
> I was afraid to tell Mrs. Owl any of these worries. I was afraid that if I told her, I would be doing something wrong. I was afraid that I would make my parents start fighting again.

I decided not to tell Mrs. Owl anything about *stresses*, but then she said, "Do you know what, Della? I know that children and little dinosaurs don't like to talk about their worries and stresses if they think that talking will hurt their families. If you're worried about that, Della, I will make you a promise. I promise to keep everything you say confidential. I promise not to tell anyone unless you tell me that someone is hurting you physically or touching you inappropriately, or if you tell me that someone has killed someone. I think it would really help you, Della, to share your worries with someone," Mrs. Owl said, "and I'd like that someone to be me."

Well, I decided to trust Mrs. Owl. "My mom and dad fight and yell a lot," I said. "Once my dad pushed my mom and slapped her and even tried to choke her. Sometimes I really hate my dad!"

I thought that Mrs. Owl would be shocked at what I said. But she wasn't. Instead, she listened to me carefully. I could tell that she understood what was happening. I could tell that she understood how I was feeling.

"I bet you feel worried and scared about the way your parents fight," Mrs. Owl said. "I bet you stay home from school sometimes because you're worried that someone might get hurt."

"That's right!" I said.

"I also bet that you think it's wrong for you to feel hate for your dad," Mrs. Owl said.

"It *is* wrong," I told her. "Little dinosaurs shouldn't hate their dad or mom."

"Well, there you are mistaken," Mrs. Owl smiled. "It's very *normal* for little dinosaurs to feel hate for a parent who uses violence to express anger. But feeling the way you do is very confusing, isn't it? Because you also love your dad, don't you?"

I nodded my head "yes."

"I'm glad you decided to talk to me," Mrs. Owl went on. "I'm always happy to help young dinosaurs learn what to do about violence in their families.

"Anger is one of the many feelings all dinosaurs have. And it's okay to feel angry. But it's never okay to choose a harmful way to express anger. Some harmful ways of expressing anger are violent. Let's see if you and I can make a list of violent ways people and dinosaurs might use to express anger."

This is the list Mrs. Owl and I made:

(Show the children the copy of the following list, which you prepared prior to the session.)

- yelling
- blaming others
- breaking things
- pushing
- shoving
- kicking
- slapping
- hitting
- punching
- killing

"I think your dad is choosing violent ways to express his anger," Mrs. Owl said. "I'm not sure why he's choosing these ways. Maybe he never learned helpful ways to express anger when he was little. If that's true, then he will probably keep on choosing violent ways to express his anger until he realizes how serious the results are and decides that he wants to change his behavior. In fact, Della, your dad might need some professional help to change."

"Can't I do something to help my dad?" I asked.

"You can do some things for *yourself*, Della. And the first thing you can do is to learn what I call the three Cs. *(Have Mrs. Owl show the group the piece of posterboard or newsprint on which you printed the three Cs prior to the session. Point out each one as Mrs. Owl presents it to the group.)*

1. Children don't CAUSE their parents to use violence to express their anger.
2. Children can't CONTROL how their parents express anger.
3. Children can't CHANGE their parents' use of violence to express anger.

"No matter how your dad decides to express his anger," Mrs. Owl explained, "the three Cs can help you remember that you never cause him to use violence, even if you do something that makes him angry. It's *never your fault* that he chooses violent ways to express anger."

When I heard this, I told Mrs. Owl that I still felt hatred toward my dad when he acts violently. I said that I was afraid that maybe I didn't love him any more.

"You probably still love your dad a lot, Della," said Mrs. Owl. "You just don't like what he's doing. It's okay for you to feel upset about what your dad is doing."

I still wanted to know what I could do to help. I mean, if I couldn't control or change my dad, what *could* I do?

"You can't take care of your dad, but you can do some things," said Mrs. Owl. "You can do some things to take care of yourself when your dad is acting violently. First, you can find a SAFE place for yourself. Second, you can ask a grown-up for HELP if your dad is out of control with his violence. Third, you can learn to RECOGNIZE, ACCEPT, and SHARE your feelings. And fourth, you can choose to learn NONVIOLENT ways to express your own feelings."

Mrs. Owl was really cool. It helped me a lot to tell somebody about the violence in my home. Mrs. Owl was able to understand my worries and problems without thinking bad things about my family.

The next time we meet, I'll tell you some more about Mrs. Owl. Until then, remember, if someone you love uses violence to express anger, it's not your fault! See you later alligators! That's an old dinosaur joke.

Discussion

Lead a discussion to help group members better understand the facts—the key concepts—presented in the story. If you wish, let the children use their puppets when they speak or let them hold Della the Dinosaur or Mrs. Owl. As the group discusses, remember to use the go-around technique: go around the group, making sure that each child has an opportunity to add to the discussion. Remember the group rule that allows a child to pass. Accept all ideas and answers, explaining or clarifying information where necessary to reinforce learning. To aid the discussion, you may use questions like the following:

- Who is Mrs. Owl? (A lady who comes to school to talk to children about how they feel.)
- Why did Della's teacher want her to see Mrs. Owl? (Della was missing school, and her grades were going down.)
- Did Della like talking to Mrs. Owl at first? (At first, Della was a little uncomfortable. It took her a while to begin to trust Mrs. Owl.)
- What are the three Cs? (Children don't *c*ause and can't *c*ontrol or *c*hange a parent's choice to use violence to express anger.)

  (Take time here to help the children learn the three Cs by heart. Use the poster you made prior to the session. Read each of the three Cs and have the children repeat after you.)

- How might children think they *cause* a parent to use violence to express anger? (Children might think that a parent uses violence because the children misbehave in school, fight with their sisters and brothers, or get low grades.)
- Can behaviors like these make a parent feel angry? (Yes, but it's the parent's personal choice to use violence to express the anger.)
- How might children think they *control* a parent's violent behavior? (Try to get the parents to stop fighting; tell the parents to stop fighting; tell a parent to get professional help.)
- How might children try to *change* a parent's choice to use violence? (Try to be perfect and get good grades in school; stay out of the parent's way and not cause any trouble.)
- Will these actions ever change a parent's violent behavior? (No.)

- Instead of trying to control a parent's violence, what should children do? (Find a safe place for themselves. Get a grown-up to help if the parent is out of control.)
- What can children do about their own feelings? (Learn to recognize, accept, and share their feelings; choose to learn nonviolent ways to express their feelings.)

Even if you choose not to use the above questions, make sure the discussion underscores these concepts.

Activity

Ask the children to retrieve their precut Mrs. Owl puppets (from Activity Sheet 5). Have glue sticks or tape available. Display the sample Mrs. Owl puppet you made prior to the session. Invite the youngsters to color Mrs. Owl in any way they like. Then show them how to use glue or tape to complete their puppets. If you're working with younger children, you may need to offer help. When the children finish, collect glue sticks or tape. Have the children put their crayons in their folders and ask them to set aside their puppets for a moment.

Basic Facts

Tell the children to take out Basic Facts Worksheet 4. Either read aloud the new basic facts yourself, or have the children read them one at a time.

8. The three Cs are:
    1. Children don't CAUSE their parents to use violence to express their anger.
    2. Children can't CONTROL how their parents express anger.
    3. Children can't CHANGE their parents' use of violence to express anger.
9. The four steps children can take are:
    1. Find a SAFE place for themselves.
    2. Ask a grown-up for HELP if the parents are out of control with their violence.
    3. Learn to RECOGNIZE, ACCEPT, and SHARE their feelings.
    4. Choose to learn NONVIOLENT ways to express their own feelings.

Briefly discuss each fact, checking for understanding.

Give the children time to complete the bottom half of the worksheet by filling in the blanks. Then have the group read the facts aloud. Ask the children to put their worksheets in their folders.

Wrapping Up

Centering Exercise

Settle the children and then repeat "The Meadow" (page 75). If you wish, let the children hold their Mrs. Owl puppets as their "trusted friend." Afterward, tell the children that they may either take Mrs. Owl home today to be a trusted friend, or they may leave her in their folders.

Affirmation

Involve the group in an affirmation. Stand and join in a circle with the children, holding hands. Go around and have the children share one fact they will remember about today's session. Begin the affirmation yourself "One fact I will remember from today's session is. . . "

Closing

Remain standing in a circle with the children, holding hands, and lead the group in the closing activity. Tell the children that you're going to make a *silent* wish for the child on your right. Then, when you've made the wish, *gently squeeze* the child's hand. The child makes a silent wish for the person on his or her right, then gently squeezes that child's hand, and so on. Continue around the circle until a wish and squeeze come back to you.

Collect the folders. Fill out a copy of the Process and Progress Form (see page 225) or the Progress Notes (see page 226), if you are an experienced leader, as soon as you can after leading the session.

Session 5: Della the Dinosaur Learns About Feelings

Objectives

To help the children:

- identify four different feelings
- discover that feelings aren't good or bad, or right or wrong; they just *are*
- learn what it means to recognize, accept, and share feelings

Session at a Glance

1. Group Rules: review—1 minute
2. Centering Exercise: "The Clouds"—3 minutes
3. Feelings Check-in: color Feeling Della—5 minutes
4. Basic Facts Review—5 minutes
5. The Story—6 minutes
6. Discussion—6 minutes
7. Activity: draw a feeling (Activity Sheet 6)—9 minutes
8. Basic Facts: (Worksheet 5) read aloud; discuss; fill in blanks; read aloud together—3 minutes
9. Centering Exercise: repeat "The Clouds"—3 minutes
10. Affirmation: share something that makes you feel happy—3 minutes
11. Closing: have a silent wish and squeeze—1 minute

Preparation

- Display the posterboard copy of the group rules.
- Have the toy Della the Dinosaur, toy Mrs. Owl, and Basic Facts Posters 1-9 available.
- Add the following materials to each folder:

  - a copy of Activity Sheet 6 ("Portrait of a Feeling")

  - a copy of Basic Facts Worksheet 5

- Have each student's folder, pencil, and crayons or markers at his or her place.
- Read through the session plan before meeting.

NOTES

Background and Guidelines

In their last session, the children discovered four things for children from violent homes—four steps—they can take to take care of themselves: (1) find a safe place for themselves; (2) ask a grown-up for help if the parents are out of control with their violence; (3) learn to recognize, accept, and share their feelings; and (4) choose to learn nonviolent ways to express their feelings. This session helps the children learn what recognizing, accepting, and sharing feelings means. As you lead the children through this session, be very accepting and nonjudgmental of all the feelings they express. Children from violent families often have very intense feelings that may prove somewhat threatening to you. For example, it's not unlikely to hear a child from a violent family say vehemently, "I hate my daddy! He hits me every day, even when I didn't do anything wrong. I wish he were dead!" If you hear statements like this, don't succumb to the temptation to tell children *not* to feel a certain way. Doing so discounts and invalidates the children's feelings. Never tell the children not to feel what they say they're feeling. Instead, help the children see that they need to identify, validate, accept, tolerate, and express their anger in helpful ways.

For example, if a child who's been hit by a parent speaks of feeling angry in group, identify the feeling: "I can tell you're feeling angry"; validate it: "Most children feel angry like you do when their parents hit them"; tolerate it: "Tell me more about how angry you feel when your daddy hits you"; and encourage the child to express his or her anger in a helpful way: "Some children in your situation draw a picture of how angry they feel" or "Some children play with clay when they're feeling angry, and express their anger by squeezing the clay over and over." Leading children through this process helps them let go of their anger. Your ability to identify, accept, and tolerate the children's feelings is part of the healing and learning process for children and the therapeutic process of the group.

Many people minimize or deny their feelings, or pretend they are without feelings. Many people fear feelings. They may fear pain, being overwhelmed by their feelings, or losing control of themselves. These people may try to swallow their feelings. However, no matter how hard people try to hold them down, the feelings don't go away. Sometimes they show themselves in physical aches and pains (somatizing). Other times they get expressed through external acting out (fighting, disrespect, delinquent behavior). Or, they may be expressed internally (depression, suicidal thoughts).

Many people who try to avoid feelings do so thinking that feelings are permanent. They are not. Unfortunately, many people often behave or take action based on this misconception. For instance, very depressed people may attempt suicide because they believe that their depression is a permanent condition. Feelings, however, are temporary. Children need to understand that they can learn to tolerate uncomfortable feelings until they pass or until they can do something to make themselves feel better. Session 2 laid the groundwork for this.

In this session, the children learn that feelings are natural and normal, and that they shouldn't be judgmental about the way they feel. At the same time, the children also begin to understand that they can be responsible for the way they express their feelings. They can use some feelings to work for them; they can express other feelings so they can let them go. Session 6 will further develop these concepts.

As you lead the children through this session, keep in mind that a particular emotion can be said to possess three components: feeling, thinking, and behavior. Children can't control the feelings they get, but they are able to control their behavior. Sometimes, examining their thinking can help children control behavior. For example, children may feel sad because their parents are sad. Seeing the sadness of their parents, children think (or "self-talk"): "I can't be happy if my parents are sad." Their behavior might be crying or withdrawing into inactivity. But children can examine their thinking and change their self-talk: "I can't be responsible for the way my parents feel. My parents feel sad, but I don't have to feel sad. I'm different from my parents. I'm responsible for my feelings. If I do feel sad, I can choose to do something to help me feel better (play a game, read, listen to music, exercise)."

This session simplifies the identification, validation, acceptance, toleration, and expression process for the children. They learn that instead of swallowing their feelings, it's better for them to recognize, accept, and share their feelings with someone they trust. With your help, the children can discover (1) words to recognize and identify (name) their feelings; (2) how to accept their feelings (remember, feelings aren't right or wrong—they just are); and (3) appropriate ways to express their feelings.

Beginning the Session

Group Rules

Welcome the children, and begin with a quick review of the group rules. Draw attention to the poster listing the group rules. If you feel that it is necessary, read the rules aloud, or call on different children to read them, one at a time.

1. I will keep what we talk about private.
   We call this confidentiality.
2. I will stay in my seat.
3. I will keep my hands to myself.
4. I will wait for my turn to talk,
   and I will listen carefully when others talk.
5. I won't tease or put other people down.

6. I can "pass" during go-arounds.
7. I will come to every group session.
8. I will make up any class work I miss.

Check for understanding before moving on.

Centering Exercise

Lead the children in a new centering exercise, "The Clouds."

Close your eyes and relax. This centering exercise can help you learn how to handle your feelings.

You're in the middle of a large playground. It's a wonderful place, in the middle of a big, open field. There's lots of space to play and run around. After playing for a while, you lie down on the soft, green grass. You're feeling happy.

Look up and see a blue sky dotted with clouds. Pretend that you're the sky and that those clouds are like the feelings you have. Watch the clouds move across the sky. See how they come and go. They're like your feelings. They come and go, too, like clouds in the sky.

Look what's coming now. It's a big storm cloud, filling the sky. It's filled with thunder and lightning. Your feeling of anger is like that cloud. It's a loud, crashing, shocking, scary feeling! But look! That big storm cloud is going away. The sun begins to shine, and the sky is bright blue again.

Slowly, a rain cloud approaches. Soon it's raining—first just a few drops; then it rains harder. The sky looks gray and sad. Before you know it, a heavy, steady rain is falling. You remember how you felt when your best friend moved away, or when a pet died, or maybe even when a grandma or grandpa died. You felt sad like the clouds in a rainy sky. But the rain cloud doesn't last forever, just like sadness doesn't last forever. Soon the rain stops. The sky turns from gray to blue once again.

Now imagine that you're back home. You're in your bedroom. It's the middle of the night. You look up to the ceiling and a magic window opens up so you can see the night sky. The wind is blowing. The moon is shining. Lots of clouds fill the sky. These are scary clouds. They make strange and frightening shapes against the moonlight. These clouds are like your feelings of being scared or worried or afraid. But listen. The wind is dying down. The scary clouds are going away. Look! The moon is shining. You fall back asleep.

Now you're back on the playground. The sky above is blue and beautiful. The clouds in the sky are white and fluffy, like big marshmallows. They go dancing across the sky. These clouds are like feelings of happiness, cheerfulness, or even love. They make you feel warm and happy inside. They put a smile on your face. But these clouds drift away, too. Soon, the sky is blue and clear once more.

Your feelings are like clouds in the sky. They come, just like clouds do. Sooner or later, they go away, just like the clouds.

Feelings Check-in

Do a feelings check-in with the children. Have them take their crayons and Feeling Dellas out of their folders. Direct the children to color in the section on Della that shows how they're feeling today. For younger children, read the names of the feelings aloud (Angry [red], Scared [purple], Sad [blue], Glad [yellow]). The children can color in more than one feeling, since it's possible to have more than one feeling at a time. Tell the children that if they're having a feeling that is not named, they can add a dinosaur spine to Della in any color they choose. Also point out that if they need to, the children can re-color a space.

When the children finish coloring, have a go-around. Begin by sharing your own feelings. Invite each child to say his or her name and to show with the Feeling Della how he or she is feeling. Be sure to accept each child's feeling(s) and to affirm each child. Ask the children to return the Feeling Dellas to their folders.

Basic Facts Review

To help the children review the basic facts learned so far, show them Basic Facts Posters 1-9:

1. People in families have many kinds of FEELINGS, and all of these feelings are normal.
2. Some ways of showing feelings are HELPFUL; some ways of showing feelings are HARMFUL.
3. Some people choose to use VIOLENT ways to express their anger. They may yell, blame, throw, break, push, shove, kick, slap, hit, punch, or kill.
4. It is NEVER okay to use violent ways to express ANGER.
5. People can choose to learn NONVIOLENT and HELPFUL ways to express their anger.
6. Parents usually LOVE their children, even when parents are choosing to use violent ways to express their anger.
7. Children usually LOVE their parents, although they may feel HATE for the parents if the parents are using violent ways to express their anger.

8. The three Cs are:
   1. Children don't CAUSE their parents to use violence to express their anger.
   2. Children can't CONTROL how their parents express anger.
   3. Children can't CHANGE their parents' use of violence to express anger.
9. The four steps children can take are:
   1. Find a SAFE place for themselves.
   2. Ask a grown-up for HELP if the parents are out of control with their violence.
   3. Learn to RECOGNIZE, ACCEPT, and SHARE their feelings.
   4. Choose to learn NONVIOLENT ways to express their own feelings.

In a go-around, ask a child to read the first fact aloud and to explain what it means. If a youngster has trouble, don't contradict or judge, simply clarify the explanation. Then ask all the children to repeat the fact together. Repeat the process for each fact.

Exploring the Story

The Story

Have the children get comfortable to listen to today's story. Invite them to hold onto their Della the Dinosaur and Mrs. Owl puppets as they listen. Use the Della the Dinosaur and Mrs. Owl toys to tell the story.

> Hi, kids. The last time I saw you, I told you about how Mrs. Owl helped me learn the three Cs. She also told me about four steps I can take for myself. I can:
>
> 1. Find a safe place for myself.
> 2. Ask a grown-up for help if my parents are out of control with their violence.
> 3. Learn to recognize, accept, and share my feelings.
> 4. Choose to learn nonviolent ways to express my feelings.
>
> Mrs. Owl taught me that it's okay to ask for help, and that one way to get help is to have someone help me learn about feelings. You see, I was having a whole bunch of feelings about my family, but I didn't really know what they were. Mrs. Owl helped me *recognize* my feelings, *accept* my feelings, and *share* my feelings.
>
> "Now, Della," she said, "recognizing feelings just means being able to name them. Accepting feelings just means telling yourself that it's okay to have them—no matter what they are. And sharing feelings just means telling someone you trust how you feel.

"Feelings aren't good or bad," said Mrs. Owl. "Feelings just ARE."

Mrs. Owl helped me recognize and accept the different kinds of feelings I was having about my family. Here are some of those feelings:

I never knew when my dad was going to be violent, so most of the time I felt WORRIED.

When I thought that my mom was going to leave my dad and get a divorce, I felt UPSET.

When my dad hit my mom, I felt HURT, because I love my mom.

I felt SCARED that my dad might hurt me.

I felt ANGRY because sometimes my dad is so violent with us, and I can't stop him.

When my dad tried to choke my mom, I felt like I HATED him, but at the same time, I felt CONFUSED because I also love him.

When my dad was calm and we went on picnics together, I felt HAPPY.

Mrs. Owl said, "Della, if you don't learn to share your feelings with someone you trust, it's like swallowing your feelings whole! It's like hiding them inside, pretending that you don't have them. If you do that, sooner or later you could become like a volcano and explode, or you might become like a plant that gets so sad it just withers and dies. You don't want either of those things to happen, do you, Della?"

"No way!" I said.

"Good," said Mrs. Owl. "Then you'd better learn this neat trick. Imagine you're in a meadow with a very good friend. Begin to experience a feeling—like anger or sadness or fear. Okay, now tell your very good friend about the feeling you're having. Feel that feeling in your body. Then pound your feet on the ground, or cry, or shake. Afterward, let yourself feel released—like you've let that feeling go. Now you feel calm and peaceful."

I tried what Mrs. Owl said. I imagined I was talking to my stuffed toy alligator, Ferdinand. I told him how sad I was. I cried with him. Afterward, I really did feel very peaceful.

Later on, I was even able to tell Mrs. Owl about my feelings. Soon I began to feel like a happy dinosaur again.

I hope that soon you'll be able to recognize, accept, and share your feelings with someone you trust, too. Take it from me, Della the Dinosaur, it really works.

Discussion

Lead a discussion to help group members better understand the facts—the key concepts—presented in the story. If you wish, let the children use their puppets when they speak or let them hold Della the Dinosaur or Mrs. Owl. As the group discusses, remember to use the go-around technique: go around the group, making sure that each child has an opportunity to add to the discussion. Remember the group rule that allows a child to pass. Accept all ideas and answers, explaining or clarifying information where necessary to reinforce learning. To aid the discussion, you may use questions like the following:

- What does it mean to *recognize* feelings? (To know what you're feeling and to name the feeling.)
- What are the names of some feelings that Della had? (Worried, upset, hurt, scared, confused, hatred, angry, happy.)
- What does it mean to *accept* feelings? (To tell yourself that no matter what you're feeling, it's okay to have that feeling.)
- What does it mean to swallow a feeling? (To pretend that you don't have it; to hide it inside.)
- What happens when you swallow feelings? (You might feel sick or sad or "explode" and hurt someone.)
- What do you think are some ways we could share feelings? (Look for answers like the following: talk to someone; write a story; draw a picture.)
- Are some feelings "good" and some feelings "bad"? (No. Feelings simply *are*.)

Even if you choose not to use the above questions, make sure the discussion underscores these concepts.

Activity

Ask the children to retrieve their copies of Activity Sheet 6. Have the children draw a picture of one kind of feeling. They can use their imaginations to draw the feeling any way they like. Again, assure the children that they need not make "perfect" drawings, since there is no "right" way to draw a feeling. If a child refuses to draw, give him or her the option to write.

When the children finish, have another go-around. Invite each child to explain his or her drawing to the group. Afterward, have the children put their crayons and drawings in their folders.

Basic Facts

Tell the children to take out Basic Facts Worksheet 5. Either read aloud the new basic facts yourself, or have the children read them one at a time.

10. Feelings aren't good or bad, right or wrong, they just ARE.
11. Instead of swallowing feelings, it's better to RECOGNIZE them, ACCEPT them, and SHARE them with someone you trust.

Briefly discuss each fact, checking for understanding.

Give the children time to complete the bottom half of the worksheet by filling in the blanks. Then have the group read the facts aloud. Ask the children to put their worksheets in their folders.

Wrapping Up

Centering Exercise

Settle the children and then repeat "The Clouds" (page 88).

Affirmation

Involve the group in an affirmation. Stand and join in a circle with the children, holding hands. Go around and have the children share something that makes them feel happy. Begin the affirmation yourself: "I feel happy when . . . "

Closing

Remain standing in a circle with the children, holding hands, and lead the group in the closing activity. Tell the children that you're going to make a *silent* wish for the child on your right. Then, when you've made the wish, *gently squeeze* the child's hand. The child makes a silent wish for the person on his or her right, then gently squeezes that child's hand, and so on. Continue around the circle until a wish and squeeze come back to you.

Collect the folders. Fill out a copy of the Process and Progress Form (see page 225) or the Progress Notes (see page 226), if you are an experienced leader, as soon as you can after leading the session.

Session 6: Della the Dinosaur Talks About Anger

Objectives

To help the children:

- identify two ways to make their anger work for them
- discover what coping means
- learn three things they can do about problems they can't change

Session at a Glance

1. Group Rules: review—1 minute
2. Centering Exercise: "The Space Shuttle"—3 minutes
3. Feelings Check-in: color Feeling Della—5 minutes
4. Basic Facts Review—6 minutes
5. The Story—7 minutes
6. Discussion—6 minutes
7. Activity: draw a way to use anger to work for you by giving you power to make changes in yourself (Activity Sheet 7)—7 minutes
8. Basic Facts: (Worksheet 6) read aloud; discuss; fill in blanks; read aloud together—3 minutes
9. Centering Exercise: repeat "The Space Shuttle"—3 minutes
10. Affirmation: share one way you can make your anger work for you by making changes in yourself—3 minutes
11. Closing: have a silent wish and squeeze—1 minute

Preparation

- Display the posterboard copy of the group rules.
- Have the toy Della the Dinosaur, the toy Mrs. Owl, and Basic Facts Posters 1-11 available.
- Add the following materials to each folder:

  - a copy of Activity Sheet 7 ("Anger at Work")

  - a copy of Basic Facts Worksheet 6
- Have each student's folder, pencil, and crayons or markers at his or her place.
- Read through the session plan before meeting.

NOTES

Background and Guidelines

Anger is a common emotion. The average person feels anger twelve to fourteen times a day. Yet, many people grow up in homes where they are taught that anger is an unacceptable feeling: "Good and decent people don't get angry." In violent homes, uncomfortable feelings—like anger—are often expressed in harmful ways. Thus, most children from these homes have had no role models to show them how to express anger appropriately. As group leader, therefore, your ability to show that anger is acceptable and that there *are* ways not only to *express* it appropriately but also to use it becomes crucial for the children in your group.

In this session, the children discover that their anger is a legitimate emotion. They begin to see anger as an energy or power that they can use positively to work for them. They discover that they can use their anger to solve problems or to make powerful changes in themselves. As group leader, you can help the children by giving specific examples. To a child who has been fighting on the school bus, you might say: "If you're angry because other kids hit you on the bus, you *can't* use your anger to change *them*. But you *can* use your anger to change *yourself* and to learn how to control yourself so you don't hit back. You can use your anger to give you power to tell those kids, in a strong voice, 'Keep your hands to yourself!'" To a kindergartner whose parents fight and don't send him or her to school, you can say: "You can use your anger to take care of yourself. You can dress, eat, and go to the bus stop by yourself. Or, you can ask a relative to take you to school. You can use your anger to take care of yourself. You don't have to feel powerless and helpless."

In light of the three Cs, the children also learn there are things that make them feel angry that they can do little about. In other words, the children come to recognize that their anger may be spurred on by problems they simply *can't* solve or change. In such cases, your task is to help the children realize they can learn to cope with the problem by accepting what they can't change, by learning to express their anger so that they can let it go, and by doing something good for themselves.

For example, a child who is angry over his or her parents' divorce will be unable to do anything to change the divorce. To such a child, you might say: Remember the three Cs? Just as children can't cause, control, or change a parent's violent behavior, neither can they cause, control, or change a parent's separation or divorce. Divorce is something children just have to accept. It's a grown-up decision that children can't change. But let's talk about some helpful ways to express this anger so you can let it go. Many kids in your situation write a letter, which they don't really send, that tells their parents how angry they feel. Other kids, whose parents are divorcing, use a special pillow and punch it until they don't feel so angry. Now let's talk about how you can also do something good for yourself. Remember what we talked about in Session 2? You could visit your grandma and play cards with her, or you could play with your favorite toys." The point here is to help the children recognize that rather than remaining in anger, powerlessness, and helplessness, they can use their anger to make changes by taking care of themselves.

The idea that anger can be used as a positive force will be a new one for most of the children. Expect some misunderstanding and resistance. Be very active and accepting during the session's discussion. Acknowledge the children's ideas about ways to express anger, but gently correct and redirect any harmful ideas—especially any violent ones—that they may express. Offer specific suggestions that are geared to the age and personalities of the children. For example: "Use your anger to give you power to control yourself when someone hits you" or "Use your anger to play football with more determination" or "Use your anger to get your spelling homework started."

Leaders who have mastered the ability to use anger to make positive changes for themselves will be better equipped to present the concepts in this session. For example, leaders who are angry about their professional standing but who use that anger to take classes to improve advancement opportunities, or leaders who tend to be passive with their spouses but who use their anger to acquire the power to speak clearly for themselves, will find themselves very effective in sharing with the children.

Children from violent homes are amply supplied with anger. Teaching them how to use their anger is a great act of empowerment. This session begins the process of tapping into the power of anger. Session 7 focuses more on teaching the children a structured plan to help them choose helpful ways to express their anger so they can let it go.

Beginning the Session

Group Rules

Welcome the children and begin with a quick review of the group rules. Draw attention to the poster listing the group rules. If you feel that it is necessary, read the rules aloud, or call on different children to read them one at a time.

1. I will keep what we talk about private.
   We call this confidentiality.
2. I will stay in my seat.
3. I will keep my hands to myself.
4. I will wait for my turn to talk,
   and I will listen carefully when others talk.
5. I won't tease or put other people down.

6. I can "pass" during go-arounds.
7. I will come to every group session.
8. I will make up any class work I miss.

Check for understanding before moving on.

Centering Exercise

Lead the children in a new centering exercise, "The Space Shuttle."

> This exercise will help you learn how to use your anger so you can let go of it.
>
> Close your eyes and relax. Imagine that you work for the people who send the space shuttle into outer space. You have an important job. You put the fuel into the space shuttle—the stuff that makes it go. The shuttle is parked and ready to go. It's going on a mission to help people in the world live peacefully together. All it needs is fuel—plenty of fuel—to get going.
>
> This space shuttle uses a very special kind of fuel. It's not like the gas people put into their cars. Instead, it needs a full tank of anger—*your* anger—to get off the ground.
>
> Think of all the things that you've felt angry about today. (*Give specific examples appropriate to the group.*) Pump all that anger into the space shuttle tank.
>
> Now think of all the things that you've felt angry about this past week. Pump all that anger into the shuttle.
>
> Now think of all the things that you've felt angry about for the past year. Pump all that anger in.
>
> By now you've been able to feel a lot of the anger you've felt in the past, and you've pumped all of it into the shuttle. It's loaded with fuel. It's ready to blast off into outer space.
>
> The countdown is beginning: 5, 4, 3, 2, 1, blastoff! Look at it go! The mission is successful. You feel great because you've used your anger in a very important way. You feel free because you've been able to let go of your anger. You feel peaceful. You feel calmer and more relaxed than you've felt in a long, long time. You also feel proud because you used your anger to work for you.

Feelings Check-in

Do a feelings check-in with the children. Have them take their crayons and Feeling Dellas out of their folders. Direct the children to color in the section on Della that shows how they're feeling today. For younger children, read the names of the feelings aloud (Angry [red], Scared [purple], Sad [blue], Glad [yellow]). The children can color in more than one feeling, since it's possible to have more than one feeling at a time. Tell the children that if they're having a feeling that is not named, they can add a dinosaur spine to Della in any color they choose. Also point out that if they need to, the children can re-color a space.

When the children finish coloring, have a go-around. Begin by sharing your own feelings. Invite each child to say his or her name and to show with Della how he or she is feeling. Be sure to accept each child's feeling(s) and to affirm each child. Ask the children to return the Feeling Dellas to their folders.

Basic Facts Review

To help the children review the basic facts learned so far, show them Basic Facts Posters 1-11:

1. People in families have many kinds of FEELINGS, and all of these feelings are normal.
2. Some ways of showing feelings are HELPFUL; some ways of showing feelings are HARMFUL.
3. Some people choose to use VIOLENT ways to express their anger. They may yell, blame, throw, break, push, shove, kick, slap, hit, punch, or kill.
4. It is NEVER okay to use violent ways to express ANGER.
5. People can choose to learn NONVIOLENT and HELPFUL ways to express their anger.
6. Parents usually LOVE their children, even when parents are choosing to use violent ways to express their anger.
7. Children usually LOVE their parents, although they may feel HATE for the parents if the parents are using violent ways to express their anger.
8. The three Cs are:
   1. Children don't CAUSE their parents to use violence to express their anger.
   2. Children can't CONTROL how their parents express anger.
   3. Children can't CHANGE their parents' use of violence to express anger.
9. The four steps children can take are:
   1. Find a SAFE place for themselves.
   2. Ask a grown-up for HELP if the parents are out of control with their violence.
   3. Learn to RECOGNIZE, ACCEPT, and SHARE their feelings.
   4. Choose to learn NONVIOLENT ways to express their own feelings.

10. Feelings aren't good or bad, right or wrong; they just ARE.
11. Instead of swallowing feelings, it's better to RECOGNIZE them, ACCEPT them, and SHARE them with someone you trust.

In a go-around, ask a child to read the first fact aloud and to explain what it means. If a youngster has trouble, don't contradict or judge, simply clarify the explanation. Then ask all the children to repeat the fact together. Repeat the process for each fact.

Exploring the Story

The Story

Have the children get comfortable to listen to today's story. Invite them to hold onto their Della the Dinosaur and Mrs. Owl puppets as they listen. Use the Della the Dinosaur and Mrs. Owl toys to tell the story.

> Hi, kids! How are you feeling today? No matter how you feel, I just want to say that your feelings are okay.
>
> Do you remember the last time we met? I told you about the many different feelings I had. I told you how Mrs. Owl helped me *recognize*, *accept*, and *share* them with someone I trusted. Today I want to tell you about another time I met with Mrs. Owl. We talked about a feeling that I had every day. That feeling was anger. But when Mrs. Owl wanted to talk to me about anger, I didn't want to talk to her. I thought that she wouldn't like me if she knew how angry I felt. But I was wrong.
>
> "Anger is a very normal feeling. All little dinosaurs get angry," Mrs. Owl told me. "Dinosaurs are like people. They feel angry as often as twelve to fourteen times a day. Living in a home with someone who expresses anger violently might make a little dinosaur feel angry even more often than that. So, Della, why don't you tell me some things that make you feel angry?"
>
> So I did. Here's what I told Mrs. Owl: "First of all, I feel angry when my parents fight. I also feel angry when my parents yell at me after they've been fighting. My brother, Danny, gets angry when he gets sent to the principal's office because he karate kicks other dinosaurs at school. The other dinosaurs always start the fights by teasing him," I explained.
>
> "Anything else?" asked Mrs. Owl.
>
> "Well, yes," I said, "I also feel angry when I have a lot of homework or a big school project to do. When I'm playing chase with Joanna and Megan, the Stegosaurus twins, and they get away from me, I feel angry."

"Thank you," said Mrs. Owl. "Thank you for trusting me enough to tell me about your angry feelings. Would you like to learn some new ways to look at your anger?"

"Yes," I said. "I'd like it very much."

"Very good," said Mrs. Owl. "Now, whenever you feel angry, the first thing to do is to look at why you feel that way. Ask yourself, 'What's the problem that's making me feel angry?' Next, look carefully at the problem to see if it's one you can do something about or can change. If it's a problem you can change, then you can use your anger to work for you. You can use your anger to give you the energy or power to make changes in yourself."

"But what if it's a problem I can't change?" I asked.

"Oh, Della," Mrs. Owl answered with a pleased smile, "I'm proud of you. You've used the three Cs to remember that there are some problems that you can't change or solve. Can you tell me what the three Cs are, Della?" Mrs. Owl asked.

(Have the group join with Della in reciting the three Cs:)

1. Children don't CAUSE their parents to use violence to express their anger.
2. Children can't CONTROL how their parents express anger.
3. Children can't CHANGE their parents' use of violence to express anger.

"Good!" said Mrs. Owl. "The three Cs can help you understand that there are some problems you just can't solve or change. But, you can do something instead. You can learn how to cope with them. Coping means handling a problem you can't change or solve.

"When you're angry because of a problem that you can't change, there are three things you can do to cope with the problem:

1. ACCEPT what you can't change.
2. EXPRESS your anger so you can let it GO.
3. Do something GOOD for yourself."

Mrs. Owl stopped and smiled. "Do you understand so far, Della?" she asked. I must have had a funny look on my face, because she didn't wait for me to answer and shake my head no. Instead, Mrs. Owl just smiled again and said, "Okay, Della, let's take a new look at the things that you said made you and your little brother, Danny, feel angry. Let's see why they make you feel that way. Let's see what the problem is. Then let's see if it's a problem you can change. If you can, let's see how you can use your anger to work for you to give you the power to make changes in yourself. If it's a problem you can't change, then we'll look at ways to cope with it."

Mrs. Owl helped me see that feeling angry about the Stegosaurus twins getting away from me when I chase them is a problem I can solve. I just have to use my anger to give myself the power to run faster to catch them.

"Of course," Mrs. Owl laughed, "if you actually catch them, then you'll have another problem altogether."

Then, Mrs. Owl and I looked closely at why Danny gets angry for getting sent to the principal's office for kicking other dinosaurs. We saw that this was a problem that Danny *can* change. Maybe Danny can't change those teasing dinosaurs, but he can use his anger to change *himself.* Then he can tell those dinosaurs who tease him, "Go chase yourselves. I'm not fighting with you." Or, he can just ignore them when they tease. He can use his anger to give him the power to control himself.

Mrs. Owl helped me see that having lots of homework or a big school project is not a problem I can change, but it is one I can make better. I can use my anger to give me the power to get going on the first step of the homework or project.

Then Mrs. Owl and I looked at why I felt angry when my parents fight and when they yell at me after they fight. She said, "Della, remember the three Cs. These are problems you can't change, but you can learn to *cope* with them."

Mrs. Owl helped me see that I can *accept* these problems by telling myself, "I'm not in charge of Mom and Dad, and I can't keep them from fighting" and "They're yelling at me not because of something I've done, but because they're upset over their own fight. I can't change that." These are problems I just have to *accept.*

Then Mrs. Owl helped me see that I can *express* my anger so I can let it go. I used to express my anger by karate kicking my brother. Doing that helped me let my anger go, but it was a harmful way of expressing anger, and that wasn't okay. Instead, Mrs. Owl helped me decide to express my anger so I could let it go by punching a pillow. Mrs. Owl also told me that after I express my anger, I can *do something good for myself,* like reading a favorite book, *Encydopedia Brown*, or playing dinosaur tennis.

Mrs. Owl showed me two good ways to handle my anger. I can use my anger to give me power to make changes in myself. Or, I can express my anger so I can let it go. I tried both these ways. They really help. Maybe you could try them, too.

The next time we meet, we'll be tallying about more ways, helpful ways, to express anger so we can let it go.

Discussion

Lead a discussion to help group members better understand the facts—the key concepts—presented in the story. If you wish, let the children use their puppets when they speak, and let them hold the toy Della the Dinosaur or Mrs. Owl. Go around the group, making sure that each child has an opportunity to add to the discussion. Encourage participation, but don't force it. Remember the group rule that allows a child to pass. Accept all ideas and answers, explaining or clarifying information where necessary to reinforce learning. To aid the discussion, you may use questions like the following:

- Is anger a normal feeling? (Yes. People—and dinosaurs—feel angry as often as twelve to fourteen times a day.)
- What should you do when you feel angry? (Look at why you're feeling angry and decide if it's a problem you can change.)
- What are some problems children *can* change? (How they behave in school; how they do their homework.)
- What should you do if it is a problem you can change? (Use anger to work for you—to give you the energy or power to make changes in yourself.)
- Can you think of any ways you can make your anger work for you? (Accept all reasonable answers; for example: use anger to help you run faster, to get you started on homework or a big project, or to control yourself instead of fighting.)
- What does *cope* mean? (Learning how to handle a problem you can't change or solve.)
- What are some problems children *can't* change? (A parent's drinking, a divorce, how the parents act.)
- What should you do if you're feeling angry because of a problem you can't change? (Accept what you can't change. Express your anger so you can let it go. Do something good for yourself.)

Even if you choose not to use the above questions, make sure the discussion underscores these concepts.

Activity

Ask the children to retrieve their copies of Activity Sheet 7. Read aloud the title at the top of the sheet: "Anger at Work." Go through the directions with the youngsters, making sure they understand them. Give them time to draw a picture of a way to make their anger work for them or a way they can use their anger to make changes in themselves. The children will need your gentle encouragement during this activity. If they misunderstand or make incorrect responses, gently correct them and urge them to choose a way to make anger work for them.

When the children finish, have a go-around. Invite each child to explain his or her drawing to the group. Take time to validate the children's angry feelings and to affirm them on finding helpful ways of making their anger work for them or using their anger to make changes in themselves. The children will learn more about dealing with—managing—anger in their next session. They will learn to choose helpful ways to express anger so they can let it go. Conclude by asking the children to place their drawings and crayons in their folders.

Basic Facts

Tell the children to take out Basic Facts Worksheet 6. Either read aloud the two new basic facts yourself, or have the children read them, one at a time.

12. When children are angry about a problem they can change, they should USE their anger to give them the power to make changes in themselves.

13. When children are angry about a problem they can't change, they should:

    1. ACCEPT what they can't change.

    2. EXPRESS their anger so they can let it GO.

    3. Do something GOOD for themselves.

Briefly discuss each fact, checking for understanding. Point out to the children how they encountered these facts in today's story.

Give the children time to complete the bottom half of the worksheet by filling in the blanks. Then have the group read the facts aloud. Have the children put their worksheets in their folders, along with their Della the Dinosaur and Mrs. Owl puppets.

Wrapping Up

Centering Exercise

Settle the children and then repeat "The Space Shuttle" (page 98).

Affirmation

Involve the group in an affirmation. Stand and join in a circle with the children, holding hands. Go around and have the children share ways they can make their anger work for them by making changes in themselves. Begin the affirmation yourself: "I can make my anger work for me to make changes in myself by . . . "

Closing

Remain standing in a circle with the children, holding hands, and lead the group in the closing activity. Tell the children that you're going to make a *silent* wish for the child on your right. Then, when you've made the wish, *gently squeeze* the dhild's hand. The child makes a silent wish for the person on his or her right, then gently squeezes that child's hand, and so on. Continue around the circle until a wish and squeeze come back to you.

Collect the folders. Fill out a copy of the Process and Progress Form (see page 225) or the Progress Notes (see page 226), if you are an experienced leader, as soon as you can after leading the session.

Session 7: Della the Dinosaur Learns to Manage Anger

Objectives

To help the children:

- understand that anger management is a way to cope with anger
- learn a seven-step plan for managing anger
- discover helpful, nonviolent ways to express angry feelings

Session at a Glance

1. Group Rules: review—1 minute
2. Centering Exercise: "The Balloons"—3 minutes
3. Feelings Check-in: color Feeling Della—5 minutes
4. Basic Facts Review—6 minutes
5. The Story—8 minutes
6. Discussion—4 minutes
7. Activity: list helpful ways to express anger and illustrate one way (Activity Sheet 8)—8 minutes
8. Basic Facts: (Worksheet 7) read aloud; discuss; fill in blanks; read aloud together—3 minutes
9. Centering Exercise: repeat "The Balloons"—3 minutes
10. Affirmation: share a time when you were angry and an appropriate way to express that anger—3 minutes
11. Closing: have a silent wish and squeeze—1 minute

Preparation

- Display the posterboard copy of the group rules.
- Have the toy Della the Dinosaur, the toy Mrs. Owl, and Basic Facts Posters 1-13 available.
- For Della, print the steps of anger management (see # 14 on Basic Facts Worksheet 7) on one side of a 4″ x 8″ index card. On the other side, print the following list of helpful ways to express anger: hammer nails, punch a pillow, do jumping jacks, write in my notebook, sit in a time-out chair, run laps around my house, draw a picture of my feelings, and talk to someone I trust.
- Provide a 4″ x 8″ index card for each child. For younger children, write the list of seven anger management steps found on Basic Facts Worksheet 7 on each card. Older Children can make their own card instead of completing the Basic Fact Worksheet.
- Make a poster. Across the top, print the title, "Steps to Managing Anger." Draw outlines of seven dinosaur footprints across the poster. (For a sample, see Activity Sheet 8.) With a marker write the steps of anger management in each footprint: RECOGNIZE, ACCEPT, RELAX, THINK, EVALUATE, CHOOSE, EXPRESS. (Note: Save the poster for use again in Session 8.)
- Add the following materials to each folder:

  - a copy of Activity Sheet 8 ("Helpful Ways I Can Express Anger")

  - a copy of Basic Facts Worksheet 7

  - the 4″ x 8″ index card that you prepared listing the anger management steps for younger students and a blank index card for older students.
- Have each student's folder, pencil, and crayons or markers at his or her place.
- Read through the session plan before meeting.

NOTES

Background and Guidelines

This session presents anger management steps that function as a cognitive behavioral technique; put simply, this session helps the children create a proactive plan to express their anger in helpful ways. The plan shows the children how to put thinking *between* feeling angry and expressing anger.

As you lead the children through the session, help them become aware of the many different ways they can express their anger so they can let it go. Specific examples will be of great help: "One child I knew was angry about his parents' fighting, so he wrote them a letter, and he punched his pillow; in a little while, he didn't feel so angry" or "One time when I felt angry, I cleaned the bathroom, top to bottom. Then I went out and jogged." To help children evaluate the consequences of their expressions of anger, teach them to ask themselves: "Will this particular action be helpful or harmful?" During the session, you may notice that some children will describe harmful ways to express anger. Don't accept these harmful ways. Rather, gently encourage and redirect the children to find a helpful way of expressing their anger.

Emphasize to the children that the anger management plan is something they can use in real life: at home, on the playground, on the bus, and in the classroom. Let the children know that it's hard to change behavior right away. In fact, most people change their behavior quite slowly. Tell the children that they can help themselves change their behavior by going through the anger management steps, even *after* they choose a harmful way to express anger. Doing so can help them figure out what would have been a more helpful choice to express their anger so they could let it go. It often takes people six to ten weeks of processing the steps retroactively before they form the habit of using the plan *at the time of anger.*

Since children with behavioral problems may have difficulty in remembering the plan and its steps, and won't be able to change their behavior immediately, it's helpful to engage their teachers, principal, and student assistance team in using the plan. Work with teachers and children to set up a plan so that the children will know exactly what choices they have with regard to expressing their anger. Explosive children may benefit from a plan that includes helpful choices such as journal writing, playing with clay, drawing a picture, or sitting in a time-out chair in the office or with the guidance counselor. Help teachers to choose behaviors that will work in a particular classroom and encourage them to help the children implement their plans when they feel angry.

Beginning the Session

Group Rules

Welcome the children and begin with a quick review of the group rules. Draw attention to the poster listing the group rules. If you feel that it is necessary, read the rules aloud, or call on different children to read them one at a time.

1. I will keep what we talk about private.
   We call this confidentiality.
2. I will stay in my seat.
3. I will keep my hands to myself.
4. I will wait for my turn to talk,
   and I will listen carefully when others talk.
5. I won't tease or put other people down.
6. I can "pass" during go-arounds.
7. I will come to every group session.
8. I will make up any class work I miss.

Check for understanding before moving on.

Centering Exercise

Lead the children in a new centering exercise, "The Balloons."

In this centering exercise, you're going to experience some anger. Then you're going to express it in a helpful way. Finally, you'll be able to let it go.

Imagine that you're very, very angry. Maybe you just had a terrible fight with your brother or sister. Maybe your parents were angry with you last night and hit you for no reason. Maybe your teacher said that you were talking in the classroom, but it was really the child who sits next to you.

No matter the reason, right now, imagine how angry you feel. You feel very hot and like you have a lot of air in your chest. You're going to express that anger by blowing up some balloons.

The first balloon that you pick up is a long, red one. Start blowing into that balloon. Blow all the anger you feel in your chest into that red balloon. (*Pause.*)

Now pick up a round, blue balloon. You start to blow into it. You huff and puff. (*Pause.*)

Pick up a very big, purple balloon. Blow and blow into it. *(Pause.)* By now you're feeling a bit better. You pick up a small, yellow balloon. You blow into it. Your air has magically turned into helium. You feel much lighter because you've put all of your anger into the balloons, and you've let your anger go. You feel calm and peaceful.

Feelings Check-in

Do a feelings check-in with the children. Have them take their crayons and Feeling Dellas out of their folders. Direct the children to color in the section that shows how they're feeling today. For younger children, read the names of the feelings aloud (Angry [red], Scared [purple], Sad [blue], Glad [yellow]). The children can color in more than one feeling, since it's possible to have more than one feeling at a time. Tell the children that if they're having a feeling that is not named, they can add a dinosaur spine to Della in any color they choose. Also point out that if they need to, the children can re-color a space.

When the children finish coloring, have a go-around. Begin by sharing your own feelings. Invite each child to say his or her name and to show with Della how he or she is feeling. Be sure to accept each child's feeling(s) and to affirm each child, paying special attention to anyone who mentions that he or she is feeling angry today. Ask the children to return the Feeling Dellas to their folders.

Basic Facts Review

To help the children review the basic facts learned so far, show them Basic Facts Posters 1-13:

1. People in families have many kinds of FEELINGS, and all of these feelings are normal.
2. Some ways of showing feelings are HELPFUL; some ways of showing feelings are HARMFUL.
3. Some people choose to use VIOLENT ways to express their anger. They may yell, blame, throw, break, push, shove, kick, slap, hit, punch, or kill.
4. It is NEVER okay to use violent ways to express ANGER.
5. People can choose to learn NONVIOLENT and HELPFUL ways to express their anger.
6. Parents usually LOVE their children, even when parents are choosing to use violent ways to express their anger.
7. Children usually LOVE their parents, although they may feel HATE for the parents if the parents are using violent ways to express their anger.

8. The three Cs are:
    1. Children don't CAUSE their parents to use violence to express their anger.
    2. Children can't CONTROL how their parents express anger.
    3. Children can't CHANGE their parents' use of violence to express anger.
9. The four steps children can take are:
    1. Find a SAFE place for themselves.
    2. Ask a grown-up for HELP if the parents are out of control with their violence.
    3. Learn to RECOGNIZE, ACCEPT, and SHARE their feelings.
    4. Choose to learn NONVIOLENT ways to express their own feelings.
10. Feelings aren't good or bad, right or wrong; they just ARE.
11. Instead of swallowing feelings, it's better to RECOGNIZE them, ACCEPT them, and SHARE them with someone you trust.
12. When children are angry about a problem they can change, they should USE their anger to give them the power to make changes in themselves.
13. When children are angry about a problem they can't change, they should:
    1. ACCEPT what they can't change.
    2. EXPRESS their anger so they can let it GO.
    3. Do something GOOD for themselves.

In a go-around, ask a child to read the first fact aloud and to explain what it means. If a youngster has trouble, don't contradict or judge, simply clarify the explanation. Then ask all the children to repeat the fact together. Repeat the process for each fact.

Exploring the Story

The Story

Have the children get comfortable to listen to today's story. Invite them to hold onto their Della the Dinosaur and Mrs. Owl puppets as they listen. Use the Della the Dinosaur and Mrs. Owl toys to tell the story.

> Hi, kids. I'm glad to see you. Can you remember the last time we talked? I said that I'd be telling you more about ways—helpful ways—to express anger so we can let it go. And that is just what I'm going to do.

Mrs. Owl wanted to help me cope with the stress I feel from coming from a family where someone uses violence to express anger. Remember, stress is anything that causes you to be worried or upset.

I feel stress when my dad yells. I feel stress when he slaps or chokes my mom. I feel stress when my mom gets hurt. I feel stress when I think *I* might get hurt. I feel stress when I worry if Mom and Dad are going to get a divorce. I also worry that my dad might kill my mom. Then Dad would have to go to jail, and Danny and I would be all alone.

Sometimes I feel that it's my fault that Dad is violent. I wish I could stop him. But I can't stop him. So I feel powerless and frustrated. Sometimes I feel trapped—trapped in a cold, dark cage.

Mrs. Owl said that all of this stress was a lot for a little dinosaur. She said that it was so much stress that it became harmful stress. Then Mrs. Owl helped me turn it back into healthy stress. She began by reminding me of the three Cs. Do you guys remember the three Cs?

(Have Della lead the children in reciting the three Cs together: Children don't CAUSE their parents to use violence to express their anger; Children can't CONTROL how their parents express anger; Children can't CHANGE their parents' use of violence to express anger.)

Remembering the three Cs helped me realize that my dad's anger is not my fault. The three Cs also helped me see that I should stop trying to change my dad. So, that's what I did. I stopped trying to change him. Then, guess what? I didn't feel so trapped. I felt much less frustrated. The three Cs helped me change harmful stress into healthy stress.

Another stress that I had was my fear that I might grow up to be just like my dad. I might grow up to use violence when I got angry. My obnoxious brother, Danny, was already acting like my dad. He was always using his karate kicks on me.

"You need to learn a new way to cope with anger," Mrs. Owl said to me. "I know about a better way of coping. It's a way called anger management. It's a plan to help you handle feelings about problems you can't change. It's a plan that shows you how to handle feelings in ways that can help you. Would you like to learn how to manage your anger, Della?"

"Yes!" I said.

"Good!" hooted Mrs. Owl. "Let's begin by taking a closer look at the way you and your brother, Danny, have been coping. Now pay attention, Della, to what you do. If your dad yells at you, the first thing you do is feel angry. And that's okay. But what's the very next thing you and Danny do?"

"Well," I said, scratching behind an ear, "Danny usually karate kicks someone. Sometimes, I karate kick Danny."

"Then what happens?" asked Mrs. Owl.

"Well, Danny gets sent to the principal's office, and I get sent to my room."

"That's right," said Mrs. Owl. "You see, Della, you and Danny haven't learned how to change your harmful stress into healthy stress. Every time you start to feel angry, you rush right from *feeling* straight into *doing*. But, Della, there's something missing in your way of coping. There's something that needs to go in between *feeling* angry thoughts and *doing* violent things. That something is *thinking*. You need a plan to help you put thinking between feeling and doing. You need a plan, Della, to help you choose nonviolent ways to express anger and to change harmful stress into healthy stress."

(Display the poster entitled "Steps to Managing Anger" and point out the seven dinosaur footprints. As Della explains the following management plan, point to the name of each step.)

Mrs. Owl says that the first step in a plan for managing anger is to RECOGNIZE that I'm angry. It's like I have to say to myself, "I'm not feeling sad. I'm not feeling lonely. I'm feeling angry."

(Point to the word RECOGNIZE in the first footprint.)

The second step to take is to ACCEPT my anger. That means I have to see that anger is a normal feeling that dinosaurs and people have, and that it's okay for me to have it.

(Point to the word ACCEPT in the second footprint.)

The third step is to practice a way to RELAX. This means that I have to do something that makes me feel relaxed. You know, like breathing through my feet.

(Point to the word RELAX in the third footprint.)

The fourth step of the plan is to THINK about the different ways I could express my anger. I could kick someone or punch a pillow or slam a door.

(Point to the word THINK in the fourth footprint.)

The fifth step is to EVALUATE the consequences of the different ways I thought about expressing my anger. This means that when I think about a way to express my anger, I also have to think about what might happen next and whether it would be helpful or harmful. Like what might happen *after* I show my anger by kicking (helpful or harmful?), or what might happen *after* I show my anger by punching a pillow (helpful or harmful?).

(Point to the word EVALUATE in the fifth footprint.)

The sixth step is to CHOOSE a *helpful* way of expressing my anger.

(Point to the word CHOOSE in the sixth footprint.)

The final step is to EXPRESS my anger—to show it—in a helpful way.

(Point to the word EXPRESS in the seventh footprint.)

Look at all these steps. Let's read them together.

(As Della points to each step, encourage the children to read each aloud. Afterward, have Della point to the fourth step, THINK, and continue the story.)

Mrs. Owl and I spent a lot of time together thinking about ways I could express my anger. She asked me to make a list of things I can do when I feel angry. I'll share my THINKING list with you, if you help me EVALUATE it. For each thing I tell you, show me a *thumbs up* if you think what might happen next would be *helpful.* But show me a *thumbs down* if what you think might happen next would be *harmful.*

These are some different ways I thought I could express my anger:

1. Stomp around the house as loudly as I can. Helpful or harmful?
2. Slam every door I can find. Helpful or harmful?
3. Punch a pillow. Helpful or harmful?
4. Do jumping jacks. Helpful or harmful?
5. Hammer nails into scrap wood. Helpful or harmful?
6. Use my loudest dinosaur roar. Helpful or harmful?
7. Slam the furniture with my tail. Helpful or harmful?
8. Write in my notebook. Helpful or harmful?
9. Draw a picture of my feeling. Helpful or harmful?
10. Run laps around my house. Helpful or harmful?
11. Sit in a time-out chair. Helpful or harmful?
12. Talk to someone I trust, like a friend, a pet, or a favorite toy. Helpful or harmful?

Thanks for helping me evaluate my list for consequences of what might happen next. You helped me see that stomping, slamming doors or furniture, and roaring would be *harmful* and violent ways to express anger.

You also helped me see that hammering nails, punching a pillow, doing jumping jacks, writing in my notebook, sitting in a time-out chair, running laps around my house, drawing a picture of my feelings, and talking to someone I trust could be *helpful* and nonviolent ways to express anger. I'll be sure to remember the help you gave me.

Before I go today, I'd like to tell you about last night. Something happened that gave me a chance to practice my steps for anger management.

My dad had a fight with my mom again. Then my dad came into my room. He yelled at me because my room was messy. He called me a lazy dinosaur. I started to feel hurt. Then I started to feel all hot and sick to my stomach. I felt very angry. I wanted to call my dad stupid and give him a nasty smack with my tail.

Instead, I remembered the plan and steps for managing my anger. I recognized that I was angry and accepted that it was okay to feel that way. I was so angry I had a hard time breathing, so I practiced a way of relaxing: I breathed through my feet. Then I remembered my list. I decided to go into my room and write about my angry feelings in my notebook. After that, I told Ferdinand, my stuffed toy alligator, what my dad had done and how angry I felt. In a little while, I calmed down. I didn't feel so angry any more. Then I decided to do something good for myself, so I read my favorite book.

The plan for managing my anger really worked well last night. But Mrs. Owl warned me that sometimes I might forget to use the steps of my plan. Then I might express my anger in a harmful and violent way. But even if that happens, Mrs. Owl said that I should still go through the steps of the plan.

"It's hard for little dinosaurs to change their behavior right away, Della, but practice makes perfect," Mrs. Owl said. "If you go through the steps often enough, it'll get easier and easier for you to remember to put thinking between feeling angry and expressing your anger in harmful and violent ways. Instead, you'll be able to express your anger in helpful ways, so you can let it go."

That's why I carry this card with me.

(Note: Have Della show the children an index card that lists the steps of anger management on one side and Della's helpful and nonviolent ways to express anger on the other side: hammering nails, punching a pillow, doing jumping jacks, writing in my notebook, sitting in a time-out chair, running laps around my house, drawing a picture of my feelings, and talking to someone I trust. See Preparation section.)

On one side, I wrote the steps for anger management. There are a lot of steps, and this card helps me remember them. On the other side of the card is a list of the things I can do to express my anger in helpful ways: hammer nails into scrap wood, punch a pillow, do jumping jacks, write in my notebook, sit in a time-out chair, run laps around the house, talk to someone I trust. I keep the list with me to help me remember what to do when I feel angry, so I can express my anger and let it go. Maybe you can make a card like this.

Until we meet next time, remember, if you feel yourself getting all steamed up and angry, take the right steps to manage your anger so you can let it go.

Discussion

Lead a discussion to help group members better understand the facts—the key concepts—presented in the story. Let the children use their puppets when they speak, and let them hold Della the Dinosaur or Mrs. Owl as they share. As the group discusses, remember to go around, making sure that each child has an opportunity to add to the discussion. Encourage participation, but don't force it. Remember the group rule that allows a child to pass. Accept all ideas and answers, explaining or clarifying information where necessary to reinforce learning. To aid the discussion, you may use questions like the following:

- What were some things that made Della and Danny feel angry? (Their parents fighting; their parents yelling at them; other dinosaurs teasing Danny.)
- Is it okay for Della and Danny to feel angry? (Yes. Feelings aren't good or bad, right or wrong; they just are.)
- Did Danny express his anger in helpful ways? (No, he used karate kicks on the other dinosaurs at school.)
- What does it mean to manage your anger? (It means having a plan to help you put thinking between feeling angry and doing angry things.)
- What are the steps of managing anger or anger management?

  (Note: Allow the children to use the poster you made as they respond: recognize that you're angry; accept your anger; practice some form of relaxation; think about different ways to express your anger; evaluate consequences; choose the best way; express the anger in a helpful way.)
- What are some ways you might recognize that you're feeling angry? (Accept all responsible replies; look for examples like the following: you might get hot, blush, sweat, feel tense, breathe hard, or feel your heart beating fast.)
- How do you accept anger? (Tell yourself it's okay to feel angry.)
- What are some ways you can relax? (Practice one of the centering exercises: "Breathing Through Your Feet," "The Icicle," "The Space Shuttle.")
- What are some ways to express anger? Are they helpful or harmful? (Accept all responsible replies; encourage the group to look to the examples Della gave in the story.)
- What does it mean to choose a helpful way to express your anger? (To pick a way that doesn't harm yourself or anyone or anything else.)
- What does it mean to express your anger in a helpful way? (To go ahead and act—to do your best choice.)

- Why should you always try to express your anger in a helpful way? (So you can let go of your anger in a way that won't hurt you or anyone else.)
- Should you expect to use these steps right away? (You should try. It's hard to change behavior right away. But if you keep using the steps, even after choosing a harmful way to express anger, doing so will help you to remember to put thinking between feelings and actions. Sooner or later, you'll use the steps when you're actually angry. But it may take two or three months and lots of practice. Don't give up.)

Even if you choose not to use the above questions, make sure the discussion underscores these concepts.

Activity

Ask the children to retrieve their copies of Activity Sheet 8. Read aloud the title at the top of the sheet: "Helpful Ways I Can Express Anger." Point out the seven footprints on the sheet. Read aloud the key words for anger management, which are found inside the footprints. Direct the children to list helpful ways they could express their anger under the footprints. (Note: You may have to help younger children with writing.) Then ask them to choose one way they like and to illustrate it on the sheet.

When the children finish, have a go-around. Invite each child to read from his or her list and to explain his or her drawing to the group. Don't accept harmful ways. Instead, gently encourage the children to choose helpful ways to express their anger. Afterward, have the children put their drawings in their folders.

Ask the children to retrieve the index card you prepared from their folders. Point out the anger management steps you've written for them on one side of the card. Then give them a moment or two to copy their lists of helpful ways they could express their anger on the other side of the card. Offer help to younger children. Tell the youngsters that they can keep their card and carry it in their pocket—just as Della does. Whenever they feel angry, they should look at the card to help them put thinking between feeling and action.

Basic Facts

Tell the children to take out Basic Facts Worksheet 7. Either read aloud the two new basic facts yourself, or have the children read them, one at a time.

14. Anger management is a way to <u>COPE</u> with anger.
15. The anger management steps are:
    1. <u>RECOGNIZE</u> that you're angry.
    2. <u>ACCEPT</u> your anger.

3. Practice some <u>RELAXATION</u>.
4. <u>THINK</u> about ways to express the anger.
5. <u>EVALUATE</u> the consequences.
6. <u>CHOOSE</u> the best way.
7. <u>EXPRESS</u> the anger in a helpful way.

By this time, the children should be very familiar with these facts. Even so, spend some time going through them, briefly discussing each fact and checking for understanding. Then have the children fill in the blanks on the bottom half of the worksheet. Finally, ask the group to read the facts aloud. Have the children put their worksheets in their folders, along with their Della the Dinosaur and Mrs. Owl puppets.

Wrapping Up

Centering Exercise

Settle the children and then repeat "The Balloons" (page 109).

Affirmation

Involve the group in an affirmation. Stand and join in a cirde with the children, holding hands. Go around and have the children share a time they felt angry and a helpful way they expressed—or could have expressed—their anger. Begin the affirmation yourself: "One time that I got angry was . . . A helpful way to express my angry feeling would have been . . . "

Closing

Remain standing in a circle with the children, holding hands, and lead the group in the closing activity. Tell the children that you're going to make a *silent* wish for the child on your right. Then, when you've made the wish, *gently squeeze* the child's hand. The child makes a silent wish for the person on his or her right, then gently squeezes that child's hand, and so on. Continue around the circle until a wish and squeeze come back to you.

Collect the folders. Fill out a copy of the Process and Progress Form (see page 225) or the Progress Notes (see page 226), if you are an experienced leader, as soon as you can after leading the session.

Session 8: Della the Dinosaur Learns Other Coping Strategies

Objectives

To help the children:

- recognize that they can draw on the facts they have learned to help them cope in stressful situations
- identify coping strategies
- understand that they can't fix their parents' problems, but they can take care of themselves

Session at a Glance

1. Group Rules: review—1 minute
2. Centering Exercise: "The Waterfall"—3 minutes
3. Feelings Check-in: color Feeling Della—5 minutes
4. Basic Facts Review—7 minutes

5-7. The Story—Discussion—Activity: discover, discuss, and write coping strategies (Activity Sheet 9)—20 minutes

8. Basic Facts: (Worksheet 8) read aloud; discuss; fill in blanks; read aloud together—2 minutes
9. Centering Exercise: repeat "The Waterfall"—3 minutes
10. Affirmation: share coping strategies—3 minutes
11. Closing: have a silent wish and squeeze—1 minute

Preparations

- Display the posterboard copy of the group rules.
- Have the toy Della the Dinosaur, the toy Mrs. Owl, and Basic Facts Posters 1-15 available.
- Have available the poster "Steps to Managing Anger" that you made for Session 7. (Note: If you plan to use the optional Session 10, retain this poster.)
- Add the following materials to each folder:
  - a copy of Activity Sheet 9 ("Coping Strategies")
  - a copy of Basic Facts Worksheet 8
- Have each student's folder, pencil, and crayons or markers at his or her place.
- Read through the session plan before meeting.

NOTES

Background and Guidelines

One of the most difficult issues for children from violent families is learning to accept their inability to solve their family's problems, especially their inability to stop a parent's use of violence to express feelings of anger, or to rescue or protect an abused parent. Group leaders like you also face this dilemma. You can't solve the children's family problems, or the problems of the children themselves. You may want to. You may feel motivated to. But you can't. Accepting this is the beginning of detachment (see Background and Guidelines for Session 4).

In this session, the children begin to own the concepts and facts they've learned in previous sessions and begin to apply them to their lives. They will use the three Cs and the four steps in this session. You will need to draw on your understanding of co-dependence, detachment, and empowerment to help the children. You will also be helping them apply the basic facts in real-life scenarios.

The session helps the children begin to detach themselves from their family's problems. Because children love their parents, this is no simple task. They will need your understanding, encouragement, and reassurance that they aren't acting selfishly. They can care about others, their parents included, but they can't fix a grown-up's problems. Many at-risk children, however, really believe they can fix their parents' problems. And parents of at-risk children frequently, and misguidedly, seek help, emotional and otherwise, from their children. Such children need your help to see that only an adult can fix adult problems, and that although it's okay for their parents to need help, they should get it from another adult.

Therefore, the children should understand that when Mrs. Owl teaches Della to take care of herself, she is not counseling selfishness. Rather, she is urging self-preservation. Like Della, the children need to take responsibility for handling their feelings in helpful ways. Doing so frees them to solve problems and to cope with those problems they can't solve. Remember, living in a violent family is difficult, frustrating, and unfair. The children will feel deeply about this situation and want to change it. They can't. They can, however, refuse to accept the responsibility for a parent's violence or for its effects on the family. This frees the children of a terrible burden and lets them use their energy to achieve personal goals.

It's important to help the children recognize that although they have no power over their family's problems, they do have power to make things better for themselves. They can decide what they want to achieve and feel good enough about themselves to take steps to attain their goals. The children can begin to take care of themselves, to control their own behavior, to ask for help, to choose to do things that are good for them, and to be with people who are helpful to them.

Note that the flow of this session differs slightly from that of earlier ones. As in previous sessions, this session's second stage, *Exploring the Story*, includes the story, discussion, activity, and basic facts. However, the first three elements of this stage (story, discussion, and activity) don't function as separate elements. Rather, they are combined in a way that allows the children to draw on the story's material directly as they discuss and apply the basic facts and concepts in the story to create effective coping strategies. Therefore, as you read over the following plan, you may wish to give some extra attention to the *Exploring the Story* stage.

Beginning the Session

Group Rules

Welcome the children warmly and begin with a quick review of the group rules. Draw attention to the poster listing the group rules. If you feel that it is necessary, read the rules aloud, or call on different children to read them one at a time.

1. I will keep what we talk about private.
   We call this confidentiality.
2. I will stay in my seat.
3. I will keep my hands to myself.
4. I will wait for my turn to talk,
   and I will listen carefully when others talk.
5. I won't tease or put other people down.
6. I can "pass" during go-arounds.
7. I will come to every group session.
8. I will make up any class work I miss.

Check for understanding before moving on.

Centering Exercise

Lead the children in a new centering exercise, "The Waterfall."

> Close your eyes and relax. Pretend that you're walking on a beautiful path in the mountains. You're taking a hike down the mountain. It's October, and the sky is clear and a deep shade of blue. The air is cool, but the sun is warm. The leaves are changing colors. Look at the beautiful shades of red, orange, and yellow. Imagine what the orange and yellow leaves look like as you look up and see them like lace against the sky.
>
> You keep walking down the mountain path until you come upon a waterfall, a beautiful cascading waterfall, a stream tumbling down over huge boul-

ders. You sit on a boulder near the waterfall, and you empty your mind. You empty your mind by paying attention to the sound of the water as it rushes over the boulders and trickles down the stream. You imagine that the water is rushing over you and making you feel clean and refreshed.

As you sit quietly on the boulder, you drink in the warmth of the sun. You see leaves are floating down the stream, because, remember, it's October and the leaves are falling. You decide to put all your worries, problems, and frustrations on the leaves and to let them all float away.

So if you're worried because (*use appropriate examples specific to the children in your group, such as . . .*) you don't have your homework finished that's due today, let that worry float away on a leaf. Or, if you had a fight on the bus this morning, and you're afraid you might get suspended, put that worry on a leaf and let it float away. Or, if you feel angry over your mom's yelling at you because she didn't like the outfit you put on this morning, put that anger on a leaf and watch it float away.

Put all your worries, problems, and frustrations on leaves and watch them all float away. Soon they're all gone. When you open your eyes, you're going to be able to work hard because all your problems have floated away. You can go back and solve these problems later.

Feelings Check-in

Do a feelings check-in with the children. Have them take their crayons and Feeling Dellas out of their folders. Direct the children to color in the section that shows how they're feeling today. For younger children, read the names of the feelings aloud (Angry [red], Scared [purple], Sad [blue], Glad [yellow]). The children can color in more than one feeling, since it's possible to have more than one feeling at a time. Tell the children that if they're having a feeling that is not named, they can add a dinosaur spine to Della in any color they choose. Also point out that if they need to, the children can re-color a space.

When the children finish coloring, have a go-around. Begin by sharing your own feelings. Invite each child to say his or her name and to show with Della how he or she is feeling. Be sure to accept each child's feeling(s) and to affirm each child, paying special attention to anyone who mentions that he or she is feeling angry today. Ask the children to return the Feeling Dellas to their folders.

Basic Facts Review

To help the children review the basic facts learned so far, show them Basic Facts Posters 1-15:

1. People in families have many kinds of FEELINGS, and all of these feelings are normal.
2. Some ways of showing feelings are HELPFUL; some ways of showing feelings are HARMFUL.

3. Some people choose to use VIOLENT ways to express their anger. They may yell, blame, throw, break, push, shove, kick, slap, hit, punch, or kill.
4. It is NEVER okay to use violent ways to express ANGER.
5. People can choose to learn NONVIOLENT and HELPFUL ways to express their anger.
6. Parents usually LOVE their children, even when parents are choosing to use violent ways to express their anger.
7. Children usually LOVE their parents, although they may feel HATE for the parents if the parents are using violent ways to express their anger.
8. The three Cs are:
    1. Children don't CAUSE their parents to use violence to express their anger.
    2. Children can't CONTROL how their parents express anger.
    3. Children can't CHANGE their parents' use of violence to express anger.
9. The four steps children can take are:
    1. Find a SAFE place for themselves.
    2. Ask a grown-up for HELP if the parents are out of control with their violence.
    3. Learn to RECOGNIZE, ACCEPT, and SHARE their feelings.
    4. Choose to learn NONVIOLENT ways to express their own feelings.
10. Feelings aren't good or bad, right or wrong; they just ARE.
11. Instead of swallowing feelings, it's better to RECOGNIZE them, ACCEPT them, and SHARE them with someone you trust.
12. When children are angry about a problem they can change, they should USE their anger to give them the power to make changes in themselves.
13. When children are angry about a problem they can't change, they should:
    1. ACCEPT what they can't change.
    2. EXPRESS their anger so they can let it GO.
    3. Do something GOOD for themselves.
14. Anger management is a way to COPE with anger.
15. The anger management steps are:
    1. RECOGNIZE that you're angry.
    2. ACCEPT your anger.

3. Practice some RELAXATION.
4. THINK about ways to express the anger.
5. EVALUATE the consequences.
6. CHOOSE the best way.
7. EXPRESS the anger in a helpful way.

In a go-around, ask a child to read the first fact aloud and to explain what it means. If a youngster has trouble, don't contradict or judge, simply clarify the explanation. Then ask all the children to repeat the fact together. Repeat the process for each fact.

Exploring the Story

The Story—Discussion—Activity

Settle the children to hear the story. If you wish, invite them to hold onto their Della the Dinosaur and Mrs. Owl puppets. Use the Della the Dinosaur and Mrs. Owl toys to tell the story.

> Hi, girls and boys! I'm glad to see you here. The last time we met, we talked about anger management and learned that it is a way of *coping* with feelings of anger. Remember, *coping* means learning how to handle a problem you can't change or solve. Then we learned a seven-step plan for managing angry feelings. Let's look at the plan again.
>
> *(Display the "Steps to Managing Anger" poster made for Session 7.)*
>
> Mrs. Owl showed me that I can use the basic facts to help me handle other problems—besides feelings of anger—I can't change or solve.
>
> "You live with someone who uses violence to express anger, don't you, Della?" Mrs. Owl asked me.
>
> "Yes, I do," I said.
>
> "Well, you know," Mrs. Owl went on, "sometimes things might happen in your family that make you feel very uncomfortable. Very often, there will be nothing you can do about those things—they'll be problems you can't change or solve. *But* you can learn strategies to cope with those things. Do you know what a *strategy* is, Della?"
>
> "Unh, uh," I said, shaking my head.
>
> "A strategy is a way or plan for doing something," Mrs. Owl explained. "So, a coping strategy is a way or plan to handle a problem you can't change or solve."
>
> "Oh, I get it," I said. "Well, at least I think I get it."

"I'll tell you what, Della," said Mrs. Owl. "I'll help you figure out some coping strategies. To begin, why don't you tell me about something that might happen in your home that would make you feel very uncomfortable?"

It only took me a second to think of something that happens in my house that makes me feel uncomfortable a lot. So I told Mrs. Owl, "Sometimes, my dad and mom have terrible fights. Sometimes, my dad slaps my mom. Whenever that happens, I try to get them to stop, but then they get angry at me."

"Okay, Della, when your parents are fighting, do you think there's any way *you* can get them to stop? Now, wait, Della. Before you answer, think of the three Cs."

I did what Mrs. Owl asked. I stopped and thought of the three Cs. Let's say the three Cs together.

(Have Della lead the group in reciting the three Cs:)

1. Children don't CAUSE their parents to use violence to express their anger.
2. Children can't CONTROL how their parents express anger.
3. Children can't CHANGE their parents' use of violence to express anger.

After thinking for a minute, I answered Mrs. Owl. "No," I said, "I guess I can't stop my parents from fighting."

Then Mrs. Owl asked, "Could you change or solve the problems your parents are having?"

I remembered the three Cs again and answered, "No, children can't solve their parents' problems."

"That's right!" Mrs. Owl hooted. "You can't solve your parents' problems. Who can solve your parents' problems, Della?"

"I guess only my parents can solve their problems," I answered.

"That's also right," Mrs. Owl said. "Parents may need to ask for help, too. But they should ask another grown-up for help. Even though you can't take care of your parents, you can take care of yourself, can't you, Della?"

"Yes, I can," I said with a smile.

"Indeed, you can," said Mrs. Owl. "So let's you and I decide on some ways you can handle this problem you can't change or solve. Let's decide on some things you can do to take care of yourself."

And so we did. We decided on a *coping strategy* I could use when my parents fight. Here it is:

1. I realize and accept that I can't make my parents stop fighting. It's not a little dinosaur's job, and I wouldn't succeed anyway.
2. I'll call my uncle, Bart Brontosaurus. I can ask him to get help for my mom if I'm afraid that she'll get hurt.
3. I'll go to a safe place where I won't get hurt. I like to go to my bedroom and play "Dinosaur Detectives" with Danny.

Can you think of any other coping strategy I could use when my parents fight?

(Break here for ***Discussion*** *and* ***Activity****.)*

Lead a discussion on the first part of the story to help the children think of another coping strategy for Della. To aid the discussion, you may use questions like the following:

- What was the first problem situation Della talked to Mrs. Owl about? (Her parents fight, and her dad slaps her mom.)
- Call Della get her parents to stop fighting? (No, it's not a little dinosaur's job, and she wouldn't be successful anyway.)
- What basic fact helped Della see that she *couldn't* get her parents to stop fighting? (The three Cs, Basic Fact 8: children don't CAUSE their parents to use violence to express their anger; children can't CONTROL how their parents express anger; children can't CHANGE their parents' use of violence to express anger.)
- Even though Della couldn't solve her parents' problem, could she do anything for herself? (Yes, she could make a coping strategy.)
- What is a coping strategy? (A way or plan to handle a problem you can't change or solve.)
- What were the three parts of Della's coping strategy to use when her parents fought? (1. Realize and accept that she can't make her parents stop fighting. It's not a little dinosaur's job, and she wouldn't succeed anyway. 2. Call her uncle, Bart Brontosaurus. Ask him to get help for her mom if she's afraid that she'll get hurt. 3. Go to a safe place where she won't get hurt. Go to her bedroom and play "Dinosaur Detectives" with Danny.)
- What are some other coping ideas Della might use?

To help the children answer this final question, ask them to take their copies of Activity Sheet 9 out of their folders. Draw attention to "Problem Situation 1" on the sheet and read it aloud. Direct the children to write their ideas for a coping strategy for Della in the space provided on the sheet. (Note: You may have to help younger children with writing.) Don't object if the children use the ideas Della suggested in the story.

When the children finish writing, have a go-around, allowing them to tell what they wrote. Make sure that their suggestions reflect an understanding that children can't solve parents' problems, but that they can take care of themselves. Afterward, return to the story, where Della will set up another problem situation that calls for another coping strategy.

(Continue with Della telling the ***Story****.)*

Thanks for your strategies, guys. Maybe I'll try your ideas for coping if my parents have another fight. But don't go away yet. I had another problem situation that needed a coping strategy. So I told Mrs. Owl about it.

"Last week," I told her, "my mom asked me if she should get a divorce from my dad."

"How did your mom's question make you feel, Della?" Mrs. Owl asked.

"It made me feel sad and scared," I said. "It made me feel like I should do something to help my mom."

"I'm sure it did, Della," said Mrs. Owl. "Your mom is having a very big problem. You love your mom and your dad. You want to help them both. You want to help your mom solve her problems. And that's very nice of you, Della. But you have to remember that you're a little dinosaur. Only a grown-up dinosaur can solve a grown-up dinosaur's problems. Only your mom can solve her problem."

"Well, okay," I said, "but I still want to make my mom feel better."

"I know you do, Della," Mrs. Owl said with a sad smile, "but remember what you know about feelings. Your mom's worry or anger aren't your feelings. They belong to your mom. Only *she* can do what needs to be done to feel better. She may need to ask for help, and that's okay. But your mom needs to ask another grown-up for help."

"Okay," I said, "but can't I tell my mom how I'm feeling? Can't I tell her that I'm feeling sad for her and that I love her?"

"You most certainly can, Della," Mrs. Owl told me. "You can remember the basic facts that tell you to recognize, accept, and share your feelings. You can share them with your mom."

"And I can share them with someone else I trust, can't I, Mrs. Owl?" I asked.

"Yes, Della," said Mrs. Owl, "and you can also do something good for yourself. Never forget, Della, you have power to make things better for yourself, even if you can't fix your mom's problem. So let's you and I decide on a coping strategy to help you."

Mrs. Owl helped me with a new coping strategy. Here it is:

1. I give my mom a big hug and tell her I'm sorry that she's feeling sad. Then I tell her that I love her.
2. I tell my mom that I can't make grown-up decisions and that maybe she should talk to another grown-up.
3. I tell someone I trust that I feel sad and scared that my mom and dad might get divorced.
4. I practice a way to relax. I paint a picture in my mind of a waterfall, and I let my worries float away.

Mrs. Owl said that it's *not* being selfish to take care of myself. I still love my parents a whole bunch, just like you love yours. But little dinosaurs like me and children like you have to keep working at handling our own feelings. We have to solve our own problems. And we have to find strategies to cope with the problems we can't solve.

*(Break here for **Discussion and Activity**.)*

Lead a discussion on the second part of the story to help the children think of another coping strategy for Della. To aid the discussion, you may use questions like the following:

- What was the second problem situation Della needed a coping strategy for? (Della's mom asked her if she should get a divorce.)
- Should children help parents decide whether to get divorced? (No. It's not a child's job. A divorce is a grown-up decision. Grown-ups may need to ask for help, but they should ask and get that help from another grown-up, not a child.)
- Can a little dinosaur—or a child—ever solve an adult's problem? (No. Only adults can solve adult problems.)
- Why is it impossible for Della to make her mom feel better? (Because her mom's feelings belong to her; only she can do what needs to be done in order to feel better.)
- Is there anyone Della *can* make feel better? (Yes, herself. She can recognize and accept her feelings of sadness and fear and share them with someone she trusts. She can also do something good for herself.)
- What were the parts of Della's coping strategy? (First, give her mom a big hug and tell her that she's sorry that her mom's feeling sad and that she loves her. Second, tell her mom that she can't make grown-up decisions and that maybe her mom should talk to another grown-up. Third, tell someone she trusts that she feels sad and scared that her mom and dad might get divorced. Fourth, practice a way to relax: paint a picture in her mind of a waterfall, and let her worries float away.)

- Do you think Della is being selfish if she won't try to make her mom feel better? (Look for answers that help the children understand that it's not being selfish to take care of themselves. While children love their parents, they can't change them. They have to work at handling their own feelings, solving their own problems, and finding strategies to cope with the problems they can't solve.) Again, don't object if the children use Della's coping strategies.

Have the children look at "Problem Situation 2" on their copies of Activity Sheet 9. Direct the children to write their ideas for another coping strategy for Della in the space provided on the sheet. (Note: You may have to help younger children with writing.)

When the children finish writing, have a go-around, allowing them to tell what they wrote. Again, make sure that their suggestions reflect an understanding that only parents can solve parents' problems, and that when children take care of themselves, they're not acting selfishly, but are showing self-preservation. Afterward, return to the story, where Della will set up a final problem situation that calls for another coping strategy.

(*Continue with Della telling the* ***Story***.)

You guys have some really good ideas about coping with problem situations. Maybe you could listen to one more. It's a problem situation that comes up a lot for me.

"I worry a whole lot about my mom," I said to Mrs. Owl. "I worry so much that my dad might hurt her that I feel sick and stay home from school."

"I understand how worried and frustrated you must feel," Mrs. Owl said. "Living in a home where someone uses violence to express feelings of anger is very difficult. But you must remember, Della, that you can't control whether your mom will get hurt, just like you can't change your dad's use of violence to express anger."

"You mean I can't do anything?" I asked.

"No," said Mrs. Owl, "you can do something. Remember your basic facts. You can control your own behavior. You can decide to make things better for yourself. You can let your anger work for you by helping you go to school and working on things you can change. Let's you and I make a coping strategy to help you deal with this problem, okay?"

"Okay!" I said. Here's the coping strategy Mrs. Owl and I made:

1. I can learn that there are some problems—like my parents' problems—that I can't fix.

2. I can hope that my parents will solve their problems. Then, I can let go of my worrying. I can concentrate on the problems I can fix, like going to school.

3. Instead of wasting my energy on something I can't control, I can put my energy into something I can control, like practicing and getting better at dinosaur tennis.

Knowing the basic facts helped me make my coping strategies for problem situations. Whenever you're in a problem situation, just remember the basic facts. Then you can come up with a coping strategy to help you, too.

*(Break here for **Discussion and Activity**.)*

Lead a discussion on the third part of the story to help the children think of a final coping strategy for Della. To aid the discussion, you may use questions like the following:

- Can Della keep her mom (or her dad for that matter) from getting hurt? (No. But she can ask a grown-up for help is she's afraid someone will get hurt.)
- What can Della do with the energy she spends worrying? (She can use it to work for her. She can put her energy into something that she can control, like her dinosaur tennis.)

Have the children look at "Problem Situation 3" on their copies of Activity Sheet 9. Direct the children to write their ideas for a final coping strategy for Della in the space provided on the sheet. (Note: You may have to help younger children with writing.) Again, don't object if the children use Della's coping strategies.

When the children finish writing, have a go-around, allowing them to tell what they wrote. Affirm the children on the ways they've been putting the facts they've learned into action. Be sure to tell the youngsters to put their sheets safely in their folders.

Basic Facts

Ask the children to take out Basic Facts Worksheet 8. Either read aloud the two new basic facts yourself, or have the children read them, one at a time.

16. Children can't FIX their parents' problems.

17. Children can take GOOD CARE of themselves.

Point out that the children have already encountered these facts in today's session. Briefly discuss each fact, checking for understanding.

Give the children time to complete the bottom half of the worksheet by filling in the blanks. Then have the group read the facts aloud. Finally, ask the children to place their worksheets in their folders, along with their Della the Dinosaur and Mrs. Owl puppets.

Wrapping Up

Centering Exercise

Settle the children and then repeat "The Waterfall" (page 123).

Affirmation

Involve the group in an affirmation. Stand and join in a circle with the children, holding hands. Go around and have the children share ideas for coping strategies. Begin the affirmation yourself: "One coping strategy I can use is . . . "

Closing

Remain standing in a circle with the children, holding hands, and lead the group in the closing activity. Tell the children that you're going to make a silent wish for the child on your right. Then, when you've made the wish, gently squeeze the child's hand. The child makes a silent wish for the person on his or her right, then gently squeezes that child's hand, and so on. Continue around the circle until a wish and squeeze come back to you.

Collect the folders. Fill out a copy of the Process and Progress Form (see page 225) or the Progress Notes (see page 226), if you are an experienced leader, as soon as you can after leading the session.

Note: If you have decided to use the optional Session 10, look ahead to it now to make plans for the children's presentation. Check out school schedules and available audiences. Be ready to talk briefly about the presentation at the conclusion of Session 9 to inform the children about the times for practicing and giving the presentation.

Session 9: Della the Dinosaur Learns How to Take Care of Herself

Objectives

To help the children:

- discover that they need to make good choices
- set goals to take care of their bodies, feelings, minds, and choices

Session at a Glance

1. Group Rules: review—1 minute
2. Centering Exercise: "The Rainbow"—3 minutes
3. Feelings Check-in: color Feeling Della—5 minutes
4. Basic Facts Review—8 minutes
5. The Story—4 minutes
6. Discussion—4 minutes
7. Activity: write personal goals for caring for self (Activity Sheet 10)—10 minutes
8. Basic Facts: (Worksheet 9) read aloud; discuss; fill in blanks; read aloud together—3 minutes
9. Centering Exercise: repeat "The Rainbow"—3 minutes
10. Affirmation: share a way you can take care of yourself—3 minutes
11. Closing: have a silent wish and squeeze—1 minute

Preparations

- Display the posterboard copy of the group rules.
- Have the toy Della the Dinosaur, the toy Mrs. Owl, and Basic Facts Posters 1-17 available.
- Add the following materials to each folder:

  - a copy of Activity Sheet 10 ("My Personal Goals")

  - a copy of Basic Facts Worksheet 9
- Have each student's folder, pencil, and crayons or markers at his or her place.
- Optional: Make a poster listing Della's personal goals (see the story and Activity Sheet 10).
- Have sheets of stiff, colored construction paper and paste or glue sticks for each child.
- Read through the session plan before meeting.

NOTES

Background and Guidelines

In this session, Della models for the children how to give up responsibility for their family's problems. Della helps them learn how to assume age-appropriate responsibility for themselves by setting personal goals. The children are encouraged to take good care of themselves and make good decisions for themselves in the areas of body, mind, feelings, and choices.

As leader, you will not be recommending that the children abandon their families, leave home, and get a job. Rather, you need to encourage them to set their sights on age-appropriate responsibilities. For example, even kindergarten children can decide to eat healthy foods and go to school every day; older children can decide to try to get on the honor roll.

When you discuss goals regarding feelings, remember that children can't control the feelings they get. However, children can be responsible for what they do with their feelings. For instance, children could wallow in feelings and be overwhelmed by them, or they could decide to choose an appropriate coping strategy to deal with them, such as talking about their feelings with someone they trust or doing something that will help them feel better. Emphasize again to the children that although they can't fix their family's problems, they can do things that will help them better cope with those problems.

For each of the areas of body, mind, feelings, and choices, help the children set goals that are positive and attainable. For example, in the area of feelings, a goal such as "I will feel happy all the time" is neither positive nor attainable. A better goal would be "I will talk to a trusted friend whenever I feel frightened or upset."

The children are asked to share goals verbally because it helps them assume ownership. With positive feedback from you and other group members, sharing also empowers the children to take the steps necessary to achieve their goals.

Beginning the Session

Group Rules

Welcome the children, and begin with a quick review of the group rules, and draw attention to the poster listing the group rules. If you feel that it is necessary, read the rules aloud, or call on different children to read them one at a time.

1. I will keep what we talk about private.
   We call this confidentiality.
2. I will stay in my seat.

3. I will keep my hands to myself.
4. I will wait for my turn to talk,
   and I will listen carefully when others talk.
5. I won't tease or put other people down.
6. I can "pass" during go-arounds.
7. I will come to every group session.
8. I will make up any class work I miss.

Check for understanding before moving on.

Centering Exercise

Lead the children in a new centering exercise, "The Rainbow."

> Close your eyes and imagine that you're asleep and dreaming. In your dream, you can fly. You soar way, way up into the sky, and you decide to land on a white, fluffy cloud. You lie back and relax on that cloud as it floats lazily across the deep blue sky. You feel safe and warm. You look down and see other clouds below you. Far beneath those clouds is the world. It looks very small.
>
> You reach into your pocket and pull out all your worries and sadness. You drop them one at a time on the clouds that float below you, one worry, one sadness per cloud. Soon, the clouds change your worries and sadness into rain that falls gently to the ground. The rain washes away all the dust and dirt and reaches deep into the earth to help the plants and trees to grow.
>
> As the rain stops, you turn to see a beautiful rainbow. You float over on your cloud and sit on top of the rainbow. You smile to yourself because you know that *you* made that beautiful rainbow. Rainbows can only come *after* a rain. Without your worries and sadness, the clouds couldn't have made the rain. And there would be no beautiful rainbow now.
>
> You think to yourself, "You can never have a rainbow unless you first have a cloud and a storm."
>
> You're going to have a good day today. You're sitting on top of a rainbow!

Feelings Check-in

Do a feelings check-in with the children. Have them take their crayons and Feeling Dellas out of their folders. Direct the children to color in the section that shows how they're feeling today. For younger children, read the names of the feelings aloud (Angry [red], Scared [purple], Sad [blue], Glad [yellow]). The children can color in more than one feeling, since it's possible to have more than one feeling at a time. Tell the children that if they're having a feeling that is not named, they can add a dinosaur spine to Della in any color they choose. Also point out that if they need to, the children can re-color a space.

When the children finish coloring, have a go-around. Begin by sharing your own feelings. Invite each child to say his or her name and to show with Della how he or she is feeling. Be sure to accept each child's feeling(s) and to affirm each child. Ask the children to return the Feeling Dellas to their folders.

Basic Facts Review

To help the children review the basic facts learned so far, show them Basic Facts Posters 1-17:

1. People in families have many kinds of <u>FEELINGS</u>, and all of these feelings are normal.
2. Some ways of showing feelings are <u>HELPFUL</u>; some ways of showing feelings are <u>HARMFUL</u>.
3. Some people choose to use <u>VIOLENT</u> ways to express their anger. They may yell, blame, throw, break, push, shove, kick, slap, hit, punch, or kill.
4. It is <u>NEVER</u> okay to use violent ways to express <u>ANGER</u>.
5. People can choose to learn <u>NONVIOLENT</u> and <u>HELPFUL</u> ways to express their anger.
6. Parents usually <u>LOVE</u> their children, even when parents are choosing to use violent ways to express their anger.
7. Children usually <u>LOVE</u> their parents, although they may feel <u>HATE</u> for the parents if the parents are using violent ways to express their anger.
8. The three Cs are:
    1. Children don't <u>CAUSE</u> their parents to use violence to express their anger.
    2. Children can't <u>CONTROL</u> how their parents express anger.
    3. Children can't <u>CHANGE</u> their parents' use of violence to express anger.

9. The four steps children can take are:
    1. Find a SAFE place for themselves.
    2. Ask a grown-up for HELP if the parents are out of control with their violence.
    3. Learn to RECOGNIZE, ACCEPT, and SHARE their feelings.
    4. Choose to learn NONVIOLENT ways to express their own feelings.
10. Feelings aren't good or bad, right or wrong; they just ARE.
11. Instead of swallowing feelings, it's better to RECOGNIZE them, ACCEPT them, and SHARE them with someone you trust.
12. When children are angry about a problem they can change, they should USE their anger to give them the power to make changes in themselves.
13. When children are angry about a problem they can't change, they should:
    1. ACCEPT what they can't change.
    2. EXPRESS their anger so they can let it GO.
    3. Do something GOOD for themselves.
14. Anger management is a way to COPE with anger.
15. The anger management steps are:
    1. RECOGNIZE that you're angry.
    2. ACCEPT your anger.
    3. Practice some RELAXATION.
    4. THINK about ways to express the anger.
    5. EVALUATE the consequences.
    6. CHOOSE the best way.
    7. EXPRESS the anger in a helpful way.
16. Children can't FIX their parents' problems.
17. Children can take GOOD CARE of themselves.

In a go-around, ask a child to read the first fact aloud and to explain what it means. If a youngster has trouble, don't contradict or judge, simply clarify the explanation. Then ask all the children to repeat the fact together. Repeat the process for each fact.

Exploring the Story

The Story

Have the children settle themselves to hear the story. If you wish, let them hold their Della the Dinosaur and Mrs. Owl puppets as they listen. Use the Della the Dinosaur and Mrs. Owl toys to tell the story.

> Hi, guys! Since I saw you last, I've been working hard on handling my feelings, solving my problems, and finding strategies to cope with the problems I can't solve. I hope you've been doing the same.
>
> The first thing I do every day is remind myself that I can't control or change my dad's use of violence. I also tell myself that I can't fix my parents' other problems, either. My parents are the only ones who can fix their problems. But I sort of wondered what Mrs. Owl meant when she said that I should take care of myself.
>
> "Mrs. Owl," I asked, "when you said that I need to take good care of myself, did you mean that I should leave home and live by myself?"
>
> "Oh, no, Della," Mrs. Owl answered. "You're still a little dinosaur, and you love your family. Your place is with them. When I said that you need to take good care of yourself, I meant that *you* can do things, even though you're still a little dinosaur, that are good for you. You can take good care of your body, your mind, your feelings, and your choices. You can set goals to take care of yourself."
>
> "Goals?" I asked. "Do you mean goals like in soccer or hockey or football?"
>
> "No, not goals like that," laughed Mrs. Owl. "The goals I'm talking about are plans for things you can do for yourself. In fact, Della," Mrs. Owl went on, "why don't you see if you can set some goals to do something good for your *whole self*: your body, your mind, your feelings, and your choices?"
>
> So that's just what I did. I made a list called "Della's Personal Goals." And here it is.
>
> *(If you made a poster showing Della's Personal Goals, display it now. Then have Della go through the goals one at a time.)*

Della's Personal Goals

For My Body:

1. Eat balanced, nutritious dinosaur food. I like at least one pine tree per day, a young pine tree so I can reach it.
2. Get plenty of dinosaur exercise. I like to practice swishing my tail because it helps my tennis backhand.
3. Get plenty of dinosaur sleep.

For My Mind:

1. Go to school every day, even if I'm worried.
2. Leave all my worrying at home.
3. Work hard on my science project (How Pterodactyls Fly!).

For My Feelings:

1. Take time to have fun every day.
2. Make a new friend.
3. Write my feelings in a notebook. This will be my dinosaur diary.

For My Choices:

1. Teach my brother, Danny, what Mrs. Owl taught me.
2. Decide never to use violence to express my anger. I know how much violence can hurt everyone.

You can make good choices, too. Maybe you can make a list of your personal goals to take good care of your body, mind, feelings, and choices.

Discussion

Lead a discussion to help the children better understand the facts—the key concepts—presented in the story. Let them use their puppets when they speak; likewise, let them hold Della the Dinosaur or Mrs. Owl. As they discuss, remember to go around the group, making sure that each child has an opportunity to add to the discussion. Encourage participation, but don't force it. Remember the group rule that allows a child to pass. Accept all ideas and answers, explaining or clarifying information where necessary to reinforce learning. To aid the discussion, you may use questions like the following:

- Can children fix their parents' other problems? (No.)
- Who *can* children take care of? (Themselves.)
- Does taking good care of themselves mean that children should leave home and live by themselves? (No. It means doing things that are good for them.)
- What are goals? (Goals are plans for things you'll do for yourself.)
- What goals did Della make to take good care of her body? (To eat nutritious food, get plenty of exercise, and get plenty of sleep.)
- What goals did Della make to take good care of her mind? (To go to school every day, leave her worries at home, and work on her science project.)
- What goals did Della make to take good care of her feelings? (To have fun each day, make a new friend, and write her feelings in a notebook.)
- What are some other ways children can take care of their feelings? (Look for responses that indicate the children's awareness of their need to recognize, accept, and share their feelings, and express them appropriately.)
- What are some important choices that children have to make? (Expect answers such as whether to follow the rules at school and at home; whether to use violence to express anger; whether to use alcohol or other drugs.)

Even if you choose not to use the above questions, make sure the discussion underscores these concepts.

Activity

Ask the children to retrieve their copies of Activity Sheet 10 and pencils. Read aloud the title at the top of the sheet: "My Personal Goals." The children will write two or three goals in each category to help them take care of their whole selves: body, mind, feelings, and choices. If you made a poster detailing Della's goals, display it for the group to see.

Lead the children through the sections on the sheet, one at a time. Remind them of Della's goals as they write their own. Make sure that everyone is finished with a section before moving on to the next. (Note: You may have to help the younger children write their goals.)

When the children finish the entire sheet, have a go-around. Invite each child to share his or her goals with the group. Take time to affirm the children on their goal setting and on their growing ability and willingness to take good care of themselves.

Give each child a sheet of stiff, colored construction paper and paste or a glue stick. Tell the children to center and then paste or glue Activity Sheet 10 onto the construction paper—making a "frame" for the sheet. Have the children put the sheets into their folders. Collect the glue sticks or paste.

Basic Facts

Tell the children to take out Basic Facts Worksheet 9. Either read aloud the last basic fact yourself, or have one of the children read it.

18. Children need to take care of their BODIES, their FEELINGS their MINDS, and their CHOICES.

Briefly discuss the new fact, checking for understanding.

Give the children time to complete the bottom half of the worksheet by filling in the blanks. Then have the group read the fact aloud. Have the children put their worksheets in their folders, along with their Della the Dinosaur and Mrs. Owl puppets.

Wrapping Up

Centering Exercise

Settle the children and then repeat "The Rainbow."

Affirmation

Involve the group in an affirmation. Stand and join in a circle with the children, holding hands. Go around and have the children share ways they can care for themselves. Begin the affirmation yourself: "One way I can take care of myself is . . . "

Closing

Remain standing in a circle with the children, holding hands, and lead the group in the closing activity. Tell the children that you're going to make a *silent* wish for the child on your right. Then, when you've made the wish, *gently squeeze* the child's hand. The child makes a silent wish for the person on his or her right, then gently squeezes that child's hand, and so on. Continue around the circle until a wish and squeeze come back to you.

Collect the folders. Fill out a copy of the Process and Progress Form (see page 225) or the Progress Notes (see page 226), if you are an experienced leader, as soon as you can after leading the session.

Note: If you've chosen to do the optional Session 10, before dismissing the children, explain that in Session 10 they will make a presentation of the material they've learned so far. Tell the children how you plan to meet in order to practice for the presentation. Set up and confirm times with them.

Session 10: Group Presentation—*Optional*

Objectives

To help the children as individuals:

- demonstrate their understanding of the basic facts about helpful and harmful ways to express feelings
- grow in self esteem

To help the children as a group:

- share feelings of cohesiveness
- successfully complete a project

To help members of the audience:

- learn about helpful and harmful ways to express feelings
- become aware of some of the issues that arise from living in a family that uses violence to express anger
- recognize that help is available for those who live in a violent family

Session at a Glance

1. Group Rules: review—1 minute
2. Centering Exercise: an exercise chosen and led by the children—3 minutes
3. Feelings Check-in: color Feeling Della—5 minutes
4. Presentation: present all the basic facts—25 minutes
5. Audience Evaluation—3 minutes
6. Centering Exercise: repeat the chosen exercise—3 minutes
7. Affirmation: share what you liked or appreciated about the presentation—4 minutes
8. Closing: have a silent wish and squeeze—1 minute

Preparation

- Since the structure of this session varies from that of the other sessions, you may wish to schedule *two meeting times* to present it. Use the first time period as a practice session to help acquaint the children with the content of their presentation, to make all necessary preparations, and to practice it. Use the second time period to conduct the actual session, allowing the children to make their presentation.
- If you feel that using all eight steps as outlined in the "Session at a Glance" with an audience present would be too much or too difficult for the youngsters, use steps 1-3 with the children *alone*; then welcome in the audience for steps 4 (Presentation) and 5 (Audience Evaluation); finally, after the audience departs, do steps 6-8 with the children. You may, of course, include the audience in all eight steps of the session.
- Decide *in advance* on an appropriate audience to view the presentation. If this is the first time for such a presentation, you may wish to invite only the school principal or SAP staff. If you're an experienced leader, you may want to target a whole grade level.
- If you can't do the presentation, consider reading the Basic Facts over the P.A. or making a Basic Facts bulletin board.
- Have copies available of each of the eighteen Basic Facts Posters (see pages 203-220).
- Have the children's folders, with all their contents, available.
- If you wish, make the children copies of the optional presentation poem (see page 148), which they'll use throughout the presentation.
- Display the posterboard copy of the group rules and the Della the Dinosaur and Mrs. Owl toys.
- Optional: Clear a wall or bulletin board space in the meeting area where the children can post all eighteen Basic Facts Posters. Have pins or tape available for the children to post the posters.
- Have available the "Three Cs" poster (from Session 4) and the "Steps to Managing Anger" poster (from Sessions 7 and 8).
- Make copies of the Audience Evaluation Form (see page 223) and have pens or pencils available for audience members.
- Read through the session plan before meeting.

NOTES

Background and Guidelines

If you are concerned about having members of a confidential group stand up in front of an audience, rest assured that the purpose of this session is not to break confidentiality. Rather, it's to provide an effective prevention activity. There's a lot to do for and in this session. Planning ahead, however, will make the task less daunting. The most effective way of guaranteeing the success of the children's presentation is advance planning and practice. Basically, the presentation entails the children presenting *all* the basic facts along with simple explanation to an invited audience. You need to decide who the audience will be and make necessary arrangements in advance.

Arrange to have one of the children lead the group and the audience in a centering exercise of the youngster's choice. The centering exercise will begin and help to conclude the session. If the children are too young to lead the exercise, plan on doing so yourself.

The children present the basic facts in eight sets. If possible, try to have at least two children present a set of facts. Thus, you'll need to designate eight pairs of children to present the sets. Since you don't have sixteen children in your group, pairs of children will need to be responsible for presenting more than one set of facts. In your practice session, you can assign the children to the different sets of facts.

Use the practice session to give the children copies of the optional presentation poem, which will serve as an introductory piece to each set of facts. Teach the poem, one line at a time. If possible, help the children learn it by heart. The poem remains the same throughout the presentation until the end, when the last line changes slightly (see page 153). Note this variation on the children's copies of the poem and draw their attention to it. Show the children the copies of the Basic Facts Posters you made. For each fact the children are assigned, they'll display a poster of the fact and read it aloud. If you wish, the children can then post the poster (in sequence) in the space provided in the meeting room.

After presenting a set of basic facts, the children will explain them to the audience by responding to questions from you, sharing posters from previous sessions, and, perhaps, by role playing. To help the presentation flow smoothly, have the children sit in a row in front of the room. Then, when you call on them to present their poem or set of facts, all they need to do is stand, look at the audience, and speak slowly and distinctly. As you practice the presentation, the order and method should become clear to the children.

If your group and/or audience is made up of younger children, adjust, abbreviate, or simplify the presentation. Do your best, however, to see that all the basic facts are presented in some visual way: on a bulletin board, in handouts, or in poster form.

At the conclusion of the presentation, you will ask audience members to fill out an Audience Evaluation Form. The forms will give you important feedback and can serve as a referral source for future groups. If audience members, including teachers, identify themselves as children from violent families, be ready to refer them to available help.

The overall goal of the presentation is not to showcase group members' talents or academic abilities. Rather, the goal is to reinforce learning, to allow the group members to reach out to others, to convey a sense of hope to the audience, and to assure all that help is available to children from homes where violence is used to express anger.

Beginning the Session

Group Rules

Warmly welcome the children and their guests and begin with a quick review of the group rules. Draw everyone's attention to the poster listing the group rules. If you feel that it is necessary, call on different children to read them one at a time.

1. I will keep what we talk about private.
   We call this confidentiality.
2. I will stay in my seat.
3. I will keep my hands to myself.
4. I will wait for my turn to talk,
   and I will listen carefully when others talk.
5. I won't tease or put other people down.
6. I can "pass" during go-arounds.
7. I will come to every group session.
8. I will make up any class work I miss.

Check that all present—including audience members—understand the group rules before moving on.

Centering Exercise

Explain to your guests that every time you meet, you always begin with a centering exercise to teach ways of relaxing and to help everyone get ready to work together. Then invite the designated child to lead the exercise, for example, "Breathing Through Your Feet."

Feelings Check-in

Give the children their folders. Have them take out their crayons and Feeling Dellas. Then do a feelings check-in with the children. Direct them to color in the section that shows how they're feeling today. For younger children, read the names of the feelings aloud (Angry [red], Scared [purple], Sad [blue], Glad [yellow]). The children can color in more than one feeling, since it's possible to have more than one feeling at a time. If they're having a feeling that is not named, they can add a dinosaur spine to Della in any color they choose. Also point out that if they need to, the children can re-color a space.

When the children finish coloring, have a go-around. Begin by sharing your own feelings. Invite each child to show with Della how he or she is feeling. Be sure to accept each child's feeling(s) and to affirm each child. If the children express fear or anxiety about the presentation, validate and tolerate their feelings. Explain that many children are fearful before the presentation, but afterward, they find they like it and want to repeat it. Conclude by having the children return the Feeling Dellas to their folders.

Presentation

Introduction

With the toy Della and toy Mrs. Owl at hand, introduce the presentation using the following or similar words: "We're part of the counseling program at (name of school). We've learned some important basic facts about helpful and harmful ways to express feelings. We want to share some of what we've learned with you."

Presenting Basic Facts 1 and 2

Have the group recite the optional poem:

Everyone has feelings; they're things that no one lacks.
We've learned a lot about them; we've learned a lot of facts.
Our feelings can be happy, angry, cheerful, or depressed.
What's important about feelings is how they are expressed.

Call on the children designated to present Basic Facts 1 and 2.

1. *People in families have many kinds of FEELINGS, and all of these feelings are normal.*
2. *Some ways of showing feelings are HELPFUL; some ways of showing feelings are HARMFUL.*

Have the children display a poster of each fact, read it aloud, explain it, and then post it.

Call on group and audience members to give examples of different kinds of feelings as well as helpful or harmful ways to express each.

Presenting Basic Facts 3, 4, and 5

Move on to the next set of basic facts by having the group recite the optional poem. Then call on the children designated to present Basic Facts 3, 4, and 5.

3. *Some people choose to use VIOLENT ways to express their anger. They may yell, blame, throw, break, push, shove, kick, slap, hit, punch, or kill.*
4. *It is NEVER okay to use violent ways to express ANGER.*
5. *People can choose to learn NONVIOLENT and HELPFUL ways to express their anger.*

Have the children display a poster of each fact, read it aloud, explain it, and then post it.

Point out that people always have a *choice* with regard to how they express their feelings. Thus, people who express their feelings of anger in violent ways, choose to do so. Emphasize that it is never okay to express anger—or any other feeling for that matter—in harmful ways.

Presenting Basic Facts 6 and 7

Move on to the next set of basic facts by having the group recite the optional poem. Then call on the children designated to present Basic Facts 6 and 7.

6. *Parents usually LOVE their children, even when parents are choosing to use violent ways to express their anger.*
7. *Children usually LOVE their parents, although they may feel HATE for the parents if the parents are using violent ways to express their anger.*

Have the children display a poster of each fact, read it aloud, explain it, and then post it.

Explain to the audience that if parents use violence, children have both positive and negative feelings about them. Help the audience see that while this situation may be very confusing, it is also "normal" in families where parents use violence to express anger.

Presenting Basic Facts 8 and 9

Move on to the next set of basic facts by having the group recite the optional poem. Then call on the children designated to present Basic Facts 8 and 9.

8. *The three Cs are:*
    1. *Children don't CAUSE their parents to use violence to express their anger.*
    2. *Children can't CONTROL how their parents express anger.*
    3. *Children can't CHANGE their parents' use of violence to express anger.*

9. *The four steps children can take are:*
   1. *Find a SAFE place for themselves.*
   2. *Ask a grown-up for HELP if the parents are out of control with their violence.*
   3. *Learn to RECOGNIZE, ACCEPT, and SHARE their feelings.*
   4. *Choose to learn NONVIOLENT ways to express their own feelings.*

Have the children display a poster of each fact, read it aloud, explain it, and then post it.

Tell the audience: "Children often believe that their family's problems are their fault, that they've *caused* their parents' violent behavior: 'My mom and dad fight because I get poor grades in school.' But this isn't the case. Children are not at fault for a parent's violence. Children can't force a parent to choose violence. Parents make that choice on their own. That's why it's important for children to learn the three Cs."

Display the poster with the three Cs (from Session 4). Point out to the audience that the three Cs are included in Basic Fact 8. Use the following questions to help the children explain the three Cs:

- How might children think they *cause* a parent to use violence to express anger? (Children might think that a parent uses violence because the children misbehave in school, don't listen to parents, fight with their sisters and brothers, or get low grades.)
- Can behaviors like these make a parent feel angry? (Yes, but it's the parent's personal choice to use violence to express the anger.)
- How might children think they *control* a parent's violent behavior? (Try to get the parents to stop fighting; tell the parents to stop fighting; tell a parent to get professional help.)
- How might children try to *change* a parent's choice to use violence? (Try to be perfect and get good grades in school; stay out of the parent's way and not cause any trouble.)
- Will these actions ever change a parent's violent behavior? (No.)

After the children respond to the questions, invite them to recite from memory the three Cs and the four steps children from families who use violence can take. Point out to the audience that the four steps help children stop trying to control and change parents. Instead, they help children learn ways to take care of themselves.

Presenting Basic Facts 10 and 11

Move on to the next set of basic facts by having the group recite the optional poem. Then call on the children designated to present Basic Facts 10 and 11.

10. *Feelings aren't good or bad, or right or wrong; they just ARE.*
11. *Instead of swallowing feelings, it's better to RECOGNIZE them, ACCEPT them, and SHARE them with someone you trust.*

Have the children display a poster of each fact, read it aloud, explain it, and then post it.

Point out to the audience that swallowing feelings means hiding them inside; recognizing feelings means being able to name them; accepting feelings means telling yourself it's okay to have them; and sharing feelings means being able to tell someone else *how* you feel.

If you wish, have the children retrieve their copies of Activity Sheet 6 ("Portrait of a Feeling") and have them share their drawings or descriptions of what they think feelings look like.

Presenting Basic Facts 12 and 13

Move on to the next set of basic facts by having the group recite the optional poem. Then call on the children designated to present Basic Facts 12 and 13.

12. *When children are angry about a problem they can change, they should USE their anger to give them the power to make changes in themselves.*
13. *When children are angry about a problem they can't change, they should:*
    1. *ACCEPT what they can't change.*
    2. *EXPRESS their anger so they can let it GO.*
    3. *Do something GOOD for themselves.*

Have the children display a poster of each fact, read it aloud, explain it, and then post it.

Use examples from the stories to point out problems children can change and problems they can't change. Solicit from the children ways they can use anger to work for them (for example, to run faster, to get started on a homework project, and so on).

Presenting Basic Facts 14 and 15

Move on to the next set of basic facts by having the group recite the optional poem. Then call on the children designated to present Basic Facts 14 and 15.

14. *Anger management is a way to COPE with anger.*
15. *The anger management steps are:*
    1. *RECOGNIZE that you're angry.*
    2. *ACCEPT your anger.*
    3. *Practice some RELAXATION.*
    4. *THINK about ways to express the anger.*
    5. *EVALUATE the consequences.*
    6. *CHOOSE the best way.*
    7. *EXPRESS the anger in a helpful way.*

Have the children display a poster of each fact, read it aloud, explain it, and then post it.

Next, ask the children to display the poster entitled "Steps to Managing Anger" (from Session 7) that shows the seven dinosaur footprints. For the benefit of the audience, briefly go through the steps, using an appropriate example (see the story in Session 7) and asking the children if different ways to express anger are helpful or harmful.

Presenting Basic Facts 16 and 17

Move on to the next set of basic facts by having the group recite the optional poem. Then call on the children designated to present Basic Facts 16 and 17.

16. *Children can't FIX their parents' problems.*
17. *Children can take GOOD CARE of themselves.*

Have the children display a poster of each fact, read it aloud, explain it, and then post it.

A good way to explain these facts to the audience is to have one of the children explain the first problem situation faced by Della the Dinosaur on Activity Sheet 9 ("My mom and dad are having a terrible fight. Dad is slapping Mom"). Then either have children read aloud a coping strategy for Della from the strategy outlined in the story from Session 9 or from Activity Sheet 9. If time allows, have a few of the children role-play the coping strategy.

Presenting Basic Fact 18

Move on to the final basic fact by having the group recite the optional poem. Then call on the children designated to present Basic Fact 18.

18. *Children need to take care of their BODIES, their FEELINGS, their MINDS, and their CHOICES.*

Have the children display a poster of the fact, read it aloud, explain it, and then post it.

Explain to the audience that children from families that use violence can live good, healthy lives if they learn to make good decisions. If appropriate, the children may share some personal goals.

Concluding the Presentation

Conclude the presentation by having the group stand, face the audience, and recite the optional poem, but with a new final line:

Everyone has feelings; they're things that no one lacks.

We've learned a lot about them; we've learned a lot of facts.

Our feelings can be happy, angry, cheerful, or depressed.

We've told you all about them; we hope that you're impressed.

Have the children take a bow. Lead the audience in applause.

Wrapping Up

Audience Evaluation

Pass out copies of the Audience Evaluation Form and pens or pencils to audience members. Encourage them to spend a moment completing the form. When audience members finish writing, collect the forms, pens, and pencils.

Centering Exercise

Ask the child who led the centering exercise at the beginning of the session to repeat it.

Affirmation

Afterward, if appropriate, involve group and audience members in an affirmation. Invite everyone to stand in a circle and hold hands. Go around and have everyone share something he or she liked or appreciated about the group's presentation. Begin the affirmation yourself: "One thing I really liked about the presentation was . . . "

Closing

Remain in the circle with everyone holding hands and lead the closing activity. Explain that you're going to make a *silent* wish for the person on your right. Then, when you've made the wish, *gently squeeze* the person's hand. The individual makes a silent wish for the person on his or her right, then gently squeezes that person's hand, and so on. Continue around the circle until a wish and squeeze come back to you.

Thank the audience for their participation. Let the group members know that you are looking forward to seeing them at your next session.

Collect the children's folders. Fill out a copy of the Process and Progress Form (see page 225) or the Progress Notes (see page 226), if you are an experienced leader, as soon as you can after leading the session.

Session 11: Della the Dinosaur Says Goodbye

Objectives

To help the children:

- review all the basic facts about violent expressions of anger
- create a personal support system
- close out their group experience

Session at a Glance

1. Group Rules: review—1 minute
2. Centering Exercise: "The Waterfall"—2 minutes
3. Feelings Check-in: color Feeling Della—5 minutes
4. Basic Facts Review (Optional: Process Session 10's Presentation)—10 minutes
5. The Story—4 minutes
6. Discussion—3 minutes
7. Activity: make a Yellow Pages booklet of people who can offer support (Activity Sheet 11) —5 minutes
8. Group Evaluation—4 minutes
9. Certificates—4 minutes
10. Affirmation and Refreshments: tell what you liked best about group and share refreshments—6 minutes
11. Closing: have a silent wish and squeeze—1 minute

Preparation

- Display the posterboard copy of the group rules.
- Have the toy Della the Dinosaur, the toy Mrs. Owl, and Basic Facts Posters 1-18 available.
- Make each child a copy of All the Basic Facts (see page 222). Center and glue or paste each sheet on a piece of colored construction paper.
- Add the following materials to each folder:

  - a copy of Activity Sheet 11 ("My Personal Yellow Pages")

  - a copy of All the Basic Facts mounted on construction paper (see above)
- Have each student's folder, pencil, and crayons or markers at his or her place.
- Optional: Make a poster of Della the Dinosaur's "My Personal Yellow Pages" (see the story, page 162) to use with the children during the story.
- Use a copy of Activity Sheet 11 to make a sample "My Personal Yellow Pages" booklet for the children to use as a model.
- To help the children complete their personal yellow pages, have ready a brief list of emergency phone numbers and the numbers of local self-help or crisis agencies.
- Make copies of the Group Evaluation Form (see page 224).
- Make copies of the Group Certificate (see page 221). Complete a certificate for each group member.
- Make arrangements to serve refreshments during the wrapping-up activity. The children may enjoy fruit and juice or cookies and milk. Home-made cookies cut in the shape of a dinosaur would be a big hit.
- Read through the session plan before meeting.

NOTES

Background and Guidelines

This session summarizes the themes of the group curriculum: education about families where violence is used, correcting misconceptions, identifying, accepting, and validating feelings, and empowerment. The children review all the basic facts and evaluate their group experience.

Over the course of the group process, the children discovered that although they can't control or change their parents' use of violence to express anger or fix family problems, they can do some crucial things to help themselves. In this session, the children realize something new: they don't have to be alone as they focus on themselves. They see that not only is it okay to ask for help, but also it's healthy and smart. Children can ask for help to learn how to deal with their feelings, how to develop coping strategies, and how to learn new skills. Thus, although this session marks the end of their group experience, it helps the children see that their support system is not diminishing, but has grown and can continue to expand.

As leader, you can help the children see that the average person needs a support system of about thirty people, not just two or three. Children need to understand that they can ask for help in many different areas of their lives, and that it's perfectly okay to have different people help in different ways at different times.

The session provides the children with a number of opportunities to share what they've gained and will remember from their group experience. But, as the children leave the group, the session does more than give them an opportunity to review. Through the story, the children discover that despite all they've learned, things will happen in the future that will upset them; that's why a support system is so vital. Emphasize this important point, stressing that using their support system (their "personal yellow pages" and other sources of help) during upsetting times is a wonderful way for the children to take good care of themselves.

Note that the centering exercise is not repeated in this final session. In its place is a small ceremony where the children receive certificates for taking part in the Della the Dinosaur Group. Be sure to have the certificates ready for the children. If possible, provide some refreshments. This not only helps the children feel self-worth, but also it tells them that they should and can have some fun, that they should and can celebrate their learning.

Sometimes, the end of group sessions is a bittersweet time for children. Be ready for some of this. Don't be afraid to speak and show your appreciation for and feelings toward the children.

Beginning the Session

Group Rules

Welcome the children warmly, and begin with a quick review of the group rules. Draw attention to the poster listing the group rules. If you feel that it is necessary, read the rules aloud, or call on different children to read them one at a time.

1. I will keep what we talk about private.
   We call this confidentiality.
2. I will stay in my seat.
3. I will keep my hands to myself.
4. I will wait for my turn to talk,
   and I will listen carefully when others talk.
5. I won't tease or put other people down.
6. I can "pass" during go-arounds.
7. I will come to every group session.
8. I will make up any class work I miss.

Tell the youngsters that these are good rules for them to use in other group situations. With some adaptation, they would work well in their classrooms or at home. Thank the children for doing a good job of sticking to their rules throughout the group sessions.

Centering Exercise

Lead the children in the centering exercise, "The Waterfall."

> Close your eyes and relax. Pretend that you're walking on a beautiful path in the mountains. You're taking a hike down the mountain. It's October, and the sky is clear and a deep shade of blue. The air is cool, but the sun is warm. The leaves are changing colors. Look at the beautiful shades of red, orange, and yellow. Imagine what the orange and yellow leaves look like as you look up and see them like lace against the sky.
>
> You keep walking down the mountain path until you come upon a waterfall, a beautiful cascading waterfall, a stream tumbling down over huge boulders. You sit on a boulder near the waterfall, and you empty your mind. You empty your mind by paying attention to the sound of the water as it rushes over the boulders and trickles down the stream. You imagine that the water is rushing over you and making you feel clean and refreshed.

As you sit quietly on the boulder, you drink in the warmth of the sun. You see leaves that are floating on the stream, because, remember, it's October and the leaves are falling. You decide to put all your worries, problems, and frustrations on the leaves and to let them all float away.

So if you're worried because (*use appropriate examples specific to the children in your group, such as . . .*) you don't have some homework that's due today, let that worry float away on a leaf. Or, if you had a fight on the bus this morning and you're afraid you might get suspended, put that worry on a leaf and let it float away. Or, if you feel angry over your mom's yelling at you because she didn't like the outfit you put on this morning, put that anger on a leaf and watch it float away.

Put all your worries, problems, and frustrations on leaves and watch them all float away. Soon they're all gone. When you open your eyes, you're going to be able to work hard because all your problems have floated away. You can go back and solve these problems later.

Feelings Check-in

Do a feelings check-in with the children. Have them take their crayons and Feeling Dellas out of their folders. Direct the children to color in the section on Della that shows how they're feeling today. For younger children, read the names of the feelings aloud (Angry [red], Scared [purple], Sad [blue], Glad [yellow]). The children can color in more than one feeling, since it's possible to have more than one feeling at a time. Tell the children that if they're having a feeling that is not named, they can add a dinosaur spine to Della in any color they choose. Also point out that if they need to, the children can re-color a space.

When the children finish coloring, have a go-around. Begin by sharing your own feelings. Invite each child to say his or her name and to show with Della how he or she is feeling. Be sure to accept each child's feeling(s) and to affirm each child. Ask the children to return the Feeling Dellas to their folders.

Basic Facts Review

To help the children review all the basic facts, have the youngsters retrieve their mounted copies of All the Basic Facts from their folders. Explain that they can keep this list to remind them of the many things they've learned about chemical dependence. You may also use copies of Basic Facts Posters 1-18 in the review.

1. People in families have many kinds of <u>FEELINGS</u>, and all of these feelings are normal.
2. Some ways of showing feelings are <u>HELPFUL</u>; some ways of showing feelings are <u>HARMFUL</u>.

3. Some people choose to use VIOLENT ways to express their anger. They may yell, blame, throw, break, push, shove, kick, slap, hit, punch, or kill.
4. It is NEVER okay to use violent ways to express ANGER.
5. People can choose to learn NONVIOLENT and HELPFUL ways to express their anger.
6. Parents usually LOVE their children, even when parents are choosing to use violent ways to express their anger.
7. Children usually LOVE their parents, although they may feel HATE for the parents if the parents are using violent ways to express their anger.
8. The three Cs are:
    1. Children don't CAUSE their parents to use violence to express their anger.
    2. Children can't CONTROL how their parents express anger.
    3. Children can't CHANGE their parents' use of violence to express anger.
9. The four steps children can take are:
    1. Find a SAFE place for themselves.
    2. Ask a grown-up for HELP if the parents are out of control with their violence.
    3. Learn to RECOGNIZE, ACCEPT, and SHARE their feelings.
    4. Choose to learn NONVIOLENT ways to express their own feelings.
10. Feelings aren't good or bad, right or wrong; they just ARE.
11. Instead of swallowing feelings, it's better to RECOGNIZE them, ACCEPT them, and SHARE them with someone you trust.
12. When children are angry about a problem they can change, they should USE their anger to give them the power to make changes in themselves.
13. When children are angry about a problem they can't change, they should:
    1. ACCEPT what they can't change.
    2. EXPRESS their anger so they can let it GO.
    3. Do something GOOD for themselves.
14. Anger management is a way to COPE with anger.
15. The anger management steps are:
    1. RECOGNIZE that you're angry.
    2. ACCEPT your anger.

3. Practice some RELAXATION.
4. THINK about ways to express the anger.
5. EVALUATE the consequences.
6. CHOOSE the best way.
7. EXPRESS the anger in a helpful way.

16. Children can't FIX their parents' problems.
17. Children can take GOOD CARE of themselves.
18. Children need to take care of their BODIES, their FEELINGS, their MINDS, and their CHOICES.

In a go-around, ask a child to read the first fact aloud and to explain what it means. If a youngster has trouble, don't contradict or judge, simply clarify the explanation. Then ask all the children to repeat the fact together. Repeat the process for each fact.

Optional: If the group took part in the Presentation of Session 10, take a moment to process it with the children. Ask them what was hard and easy about the presentation, what was the most fun, what could have made it better. Record the children's observations to use and consider when presenting Session 10 in the future.

Exploring the Story

The Story

Have the children settle themselves to hear the story. If you wish, let them hold their Della the Dinosaur and Mrs. Owl puppets as they listen. Use the Della the Dinosaur and Mrs. Owl toys to tell the story.

> It's hard to believe that our time together as a group is almost finished. So before we're done, I want you to know how much you've helped me learn. I feel proud of the changes I've made. I know that I had some wrong ideas before, but now I know the facts about feelings. I know it's important for me to ask for help. I know that it's important to choose to use nonviolent ways to express anger.
>
> Can you remember when we first met? Back then I used to feel scared and worried all the time. I was so worried I would stay home from school. My grades were slipping, too. Remember how Danny was acting? He was expressing his anger by karate kicking me and everyone else. Now Danny and I both recognize our feelings. We know how to relax through exercises like "Breathing Through My Feet," "The Space Shuttle," and "The Waterfall." We use coping strategies to deal with problems we can't solve. And we follow a plan for managing our anger. I'm especially happy about that. No more karate kick bruises on my legs!

I used to be so angry all the time. Now I use my anger to work for me. If I feel angry about having a lot of homework, I use my anger to give me the power to get myself started. Or, I express my anger so I can let it go—I run into my room and punch my pillow.

I don't stay home from school anymore, and my grades are slowly getting better. Let me tell you, I feel very happy about that.

Things at home haven't changed much. My parents still fight. I never know whether it's going to be calm or stormy there. I still feel sad about that. But now I know that I didn't cause my parents to fight. I also know that I can't change or control their anger and fighting. But I also know that I *can* do things to help myself and take good care of myself, so that I can grow up to be a strong and healthy dinosaur.

Mrs. Owl is proud of me and the changes I've made. She's happy that I'm doing so much better. But she told me that not everything will always be perfect.

"Della," she said, "sometimes things in your life will bother you. That's the way life is. But, in tough times, you can always turn to others for help. Remember, you don't have to solve all your problems by yourself. You don't even have to figure out how to cope with your problems all by yourself."

"Do you mean if I have a problem with a question on a test in school that it would be okay to ask someone for the answer?" I asked.

"No, Della," Mrs. Owl answered. "When you're taking a test in school, it's not okay to ask someone else for help, but it is okay to ask someone for help in solving a homework problem. It's also okay to ask a friend to listen when you have a difficult feeling to share. And it's very much okay to have a friend to play with to make sure that you have fun every day."

"But, Mrs. Owl, who will I call if I need help?" I asked. "I know I have you for a friend, but where else can I look for help? Who else can I call?"

"Ah ha!" Mrs. Owl exclaimed. "You've given me a great idea, Della. When grown-ups need help and don't know who to call, they look in the yellow pages of the telephone book. I think you should make your own yellow pages of people you can call or go to for help whenever you're having trouble."

So that's what I did. I made my own special list of people I could call for help. I call it My Personal Yellow Pages.

(Show the children the poster "My Personal Yellow Pages," outlining Della's list of people to call for help. Have Della go through the list with the group.)

My Personal Yellow Pages

People to have fun with:

The Triceratops triplets, Mikey, Matthew, and Thomas

The Stegosaurus twins, Joanna and Megan

People to ask for help with schoolwork:

My teacher, the librarian, Leigh Brontosaurus, Dad (if he is calm)

People to talk to when I have a problem or feel sad or angry:

Mom, my grandma and grandpa, my stuffed toy alligator, Ferdinand, Uncle Bart

Safe places to go if my parents fight:

My bedroom, the park if it's daytime

Important phone numbers:

Emergency: 911

Grandpa and Grandma: 555-0001

Uncle Bart Brontosaurus: 555-2671

That's my personal yellow pages. Maybe you can make your own. Then you would know who to call or go to whenever you're in trouble and need help.

Right now, I want to thank you for *your* help. When I first met you, I wasn't feeling very well. But telling you about my family and talking about feelings has helped me understand my feelings a whole lot better. Because of the facts we've learned and friendship we've shared, I'm feeling much happier now.

I hope you've learned ways to be a healthier, happier dinosaur—Whoops! I mean person—especially if you live in a family where violent ways are used to express anger.

I suppose there are lots of different things I could say to you. But I think the best thing I can say is

Good Luck and Goodbye.

Discussion

Lead a discussion to help the children better understand the facts—the key concepts—presented in the story. Let them use their puppets when they speak, or let them hold Della the Dinosaur or Mrs. Owl. As they discuss, remember to go around the group, making sure that each child has an opportunity to add to the discussion. Encourage participation, but don't force it. Remember the group rule that allows a child to pass. Accept all ideas and answers, explaining or clarifying information where necessary to reinforce learning. To aid the discussion, you may use questions like the following:

- How has Della changed through her work with Mrs. Owl? (Look for answers such as: she has learned the facts about helpful and harmful ways to express feelings, especially anger; she has stopped skipping school.)
- What coping strategies does Della use now? (She recognizes and shares her feelings; she uses centering exercises; she remembers that she didn't cause and can't control or change her parents' choice to use anger to express violence.)
- Do you think that Della's troubles are over, that life will be perfect for her from now on? (No, that's not the way life is.)
- Is it okay to ask other people for help? (Yes. It's okay to have friends to have fun with; to ask for help with schoolwork; to have people to talk to when you have a problem or are feeling sad or angry.)

Even if you choose not to use the above questions, make sure the discussion underscores these concepts. Thank the children for taking part in the discussion. Affirm how much they've learned.

Activity

Ask the children to retrieve their copies of Activity Sheet 11. Display the sample yellow pages booklet you made prior to the session. Show the group how to fold the sheet to make their own booklets. Have the children write their names on the line at the top of the booklet's cover page. Read aloud the title on the cover, "My Personal Yellow Pages." Then go through the booklet page by page. For each page, read the heading(s), then give the children time to complete the page.

For the heading, "Important phone numbers," on the last page, you may have to offer some assistance. For example, since most communities have 911 service, 911 is *the* emergency telephone number. If, however, there is no 911 service in your area, direct the children to write in "O" for Operator or your specific, local emergency number. You might want to make available the numbers of local helping hotlines, explaining that there are caring people at these numbers who can listen and offer help.

When the children finish writing, have a go-around. Invite each child to share from his or her yellow pages. Have the children place their yellow pages in their folders. Tell them they may take their folders home with them.

Group Evaluation

Since the children have completed all the basic facts, there is no Basic Facts Worksheet for this session. Instead, pass out copies of the Group Evaluation Form and ask the children to complete it. Explain to the youngsters that their honesty will help you make the group better for other children. Point out that they need not put their names on the form. Older children may work on their own. Younger children, however, may require your assistance. For example, you may have to read each question aloud, or you may have to help with writing or spelling. When the children finish, collect the forms to use when you evaluate the group program.

Wrapping Up

Certificates

Thank the children for their hard work, sharing, and openness by calling each child forward and presenting him or her with a Group Certificate. As you present the certificates, offer a personal note of thanks, mentioning something special to each child about his or her unique contribution to the group.

Refreshments and Affirmation

Surprise the children with some refreshments. (Try those dinosaur-shaped cookies.) After the refreshments are finished, involve the group in a final affirmation. Stand and join in a circle with the children, holding hands. Go around and have the children share something that they really liked about the group. Begin the affirmation yourself: "What I liked most about this group is...."

Closing

Lead the group in the closing activity: Stand and join in a circle with the children, holding hands. Tell the children that you're going to make a *silent* wish for the child on your right. Then, when you've made the wish, *gently squeeze* the child's hand. The child makes a silent wish for the person on his or her right, then gently squeezes that child's hand, and so on. Continue around the circle until a wish and squeeze come back to you.

Say a personal goodbye to the children.

Fill out a copy of the Process and Progress Form (see page 225) or the Progress Notes (see page 226).

Part Three

Support Materials

This section of the manual includes the tools you'll need to develop and support the group program in your school. Each of the following materials is printed in blackline master form and is suitable for copying on most photocopy machines.

Group Rules Contract. You'll need a copy of this contract for every group member. The Group Rules Contract will be used in Session 1 and in the screening interview.

Feeling Della. This sheet will aid you in doing a feelings check-in with the children. Each group member will need *one* copy. The children will use their copy of Feeling Della in Sessions 2-11.

Activity Sheets. There are eleven Activity Sheets. They'll be used in the various sessions. Make sure that everyone in your group has a copy of the sheet(s) needed. It's a good idea to make extra copies in case children have problems.

Basic Facts Worksheets. The nine Basic Fact Worksheets will be used by the children in their sessions together.

Basic Facts Worksheets with Answers Dotted In. These nine worksheets have the answers dotted in to help younger group members (K-first grade) and special education populations.

Basic Facts Posters. These eighteen sheets reproduce the basic facts in large print. They can be photocopied and laminated for use in the sessions (for the Basic Facts Review and the presentation in the optional Session 10). They also can be made into transparencies for larger presentations.

Group Certificate. This award or participation certificate may be photocopied, filled out, and given to each group member during Session 11.

All the Basic Facts. The complete list of basic facts is to be copied and mounted on construction paper and given out in Session 11.

Audience Evaluation Form. This form may be used to evaluate the optional children's presentation in Session 10. It is designed to provide important feedback regarding the presentation's effectiveness and to serve as a referral source for future groups.

Group Evaluation Form. This form is to be used in Session 11 by the children to evaluate their total group experience.

Process and Progress Form. This form is for you, the group leader. Make eleven copies of the form. After each session, fill out a copy of the form in order to evaluate the session and to keep timely notes on the progress of the group.

Progress Notes. This two-page form is a more condensed version of the Process and Progress Form and is suitable for the more experienced group leader. Simply copy each page and fill out the appropriate section after each group session.

Self-Referral Group Survey Form. Designed for children grades 2 and up, this form should be made available to children after they've heard about the purpose of the support groups. Use the form in conjunction with a presentation at which available groups are explained to the children (see page 20). When the children fill out the form, explain that if they want to be in more than one group, they should number their choices in priority. Also, make sure the children know that not everyone may be in groups right away and that groups will be offered according to need and time.

Parental Consent Letter. Once children have been referred or self-referred to a group, you should seek parental consent by sending parents a copy of a letter like the one provided here.

Screening Interview Outline. After referrals are obtained and categorized, the children need to be interviewed individually. The Screening Interview Outline will help you get basic, necessary information about the children and their daily life. If children seem like appropriate candidates, be sure to explain the group format and to show them a copy of the Group Rules Contract. Make sure the children understand that they must attend every session and be willing to make up missed schoolwork.

****

This section of the manual also includes a list of professional resources for your enrichment and names and addresses of helping agencies.

Group Rules Contract

1. I will keep what we talk about private.
   We call this confidentiality.

2. I will stay in my seat.

3. I will keep my hands to myself.

4. I will wait for my turn to talk,
   and I will listen carefully when others talk.

5. I won't tease or put other people down.

6. I can "pass" during go-arounds.

7. I will come to every group session.

8. I will make up any class work I miss.

____

Name

____

Date

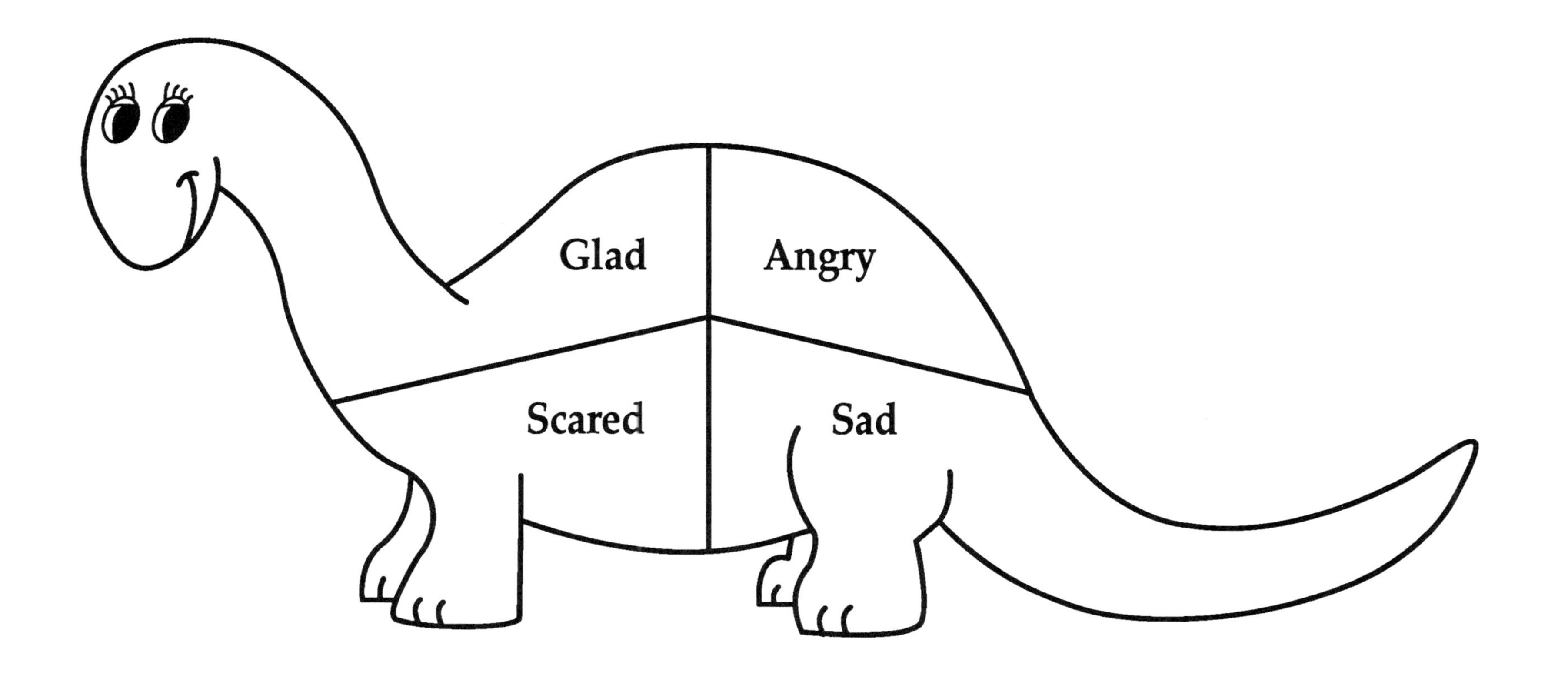

Feeling Della

Glad = Yellow   Angry = Red

Sad = Blue   Scared = Purple

Activity Sheet 1

Della the Dinosaur Puppet

Activity Sheet 2

This Person Is Angry

Activity Sheet 3

This Is What I Do to Feel Happy

Activity Sheet 4

A Feeling Picture of My Family

Draw your family.
Color each person the feeling he or she would be.

Angry [red]   Scared [purple]   Sad [blue]   Glad [yellow]

Activity Sheet 5

Mrs. Owl Puppet

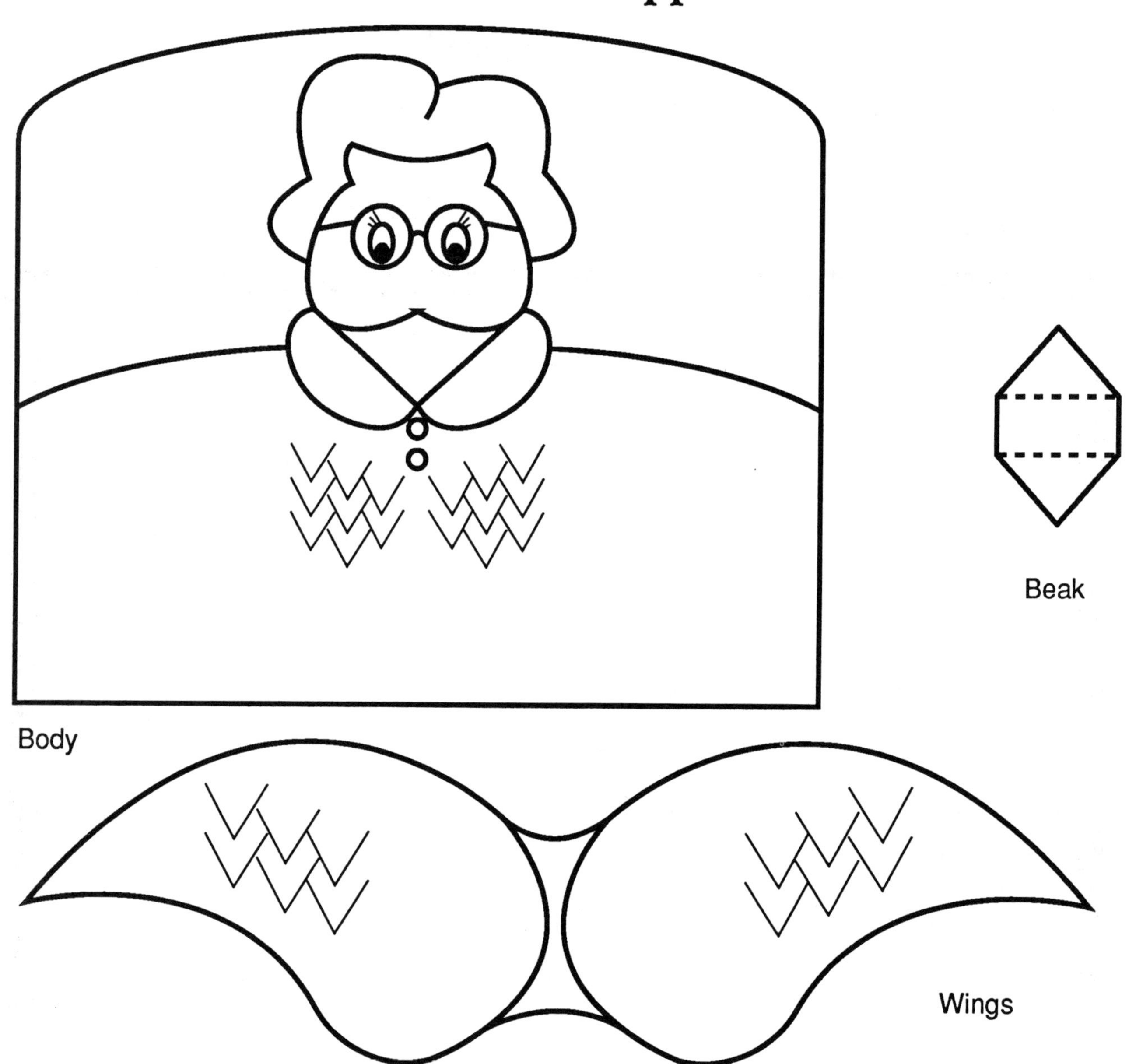

1. Color Mrs. Owl with your favorite colors. Color her beak, her body, and her wings.
2. Cut out the body. Print your name on the back.
   Roll the ends toward the back and tape or paste together.
3. Cut out the beak. Tape or paste the beak onto Mrs. Owl's face.
4. Cut out the wings. Tape or paste them onto Mrs. Owl's back.

Activity Sheet 6

Portrait of a Feeling

Draw a picture of one kind of feeling.

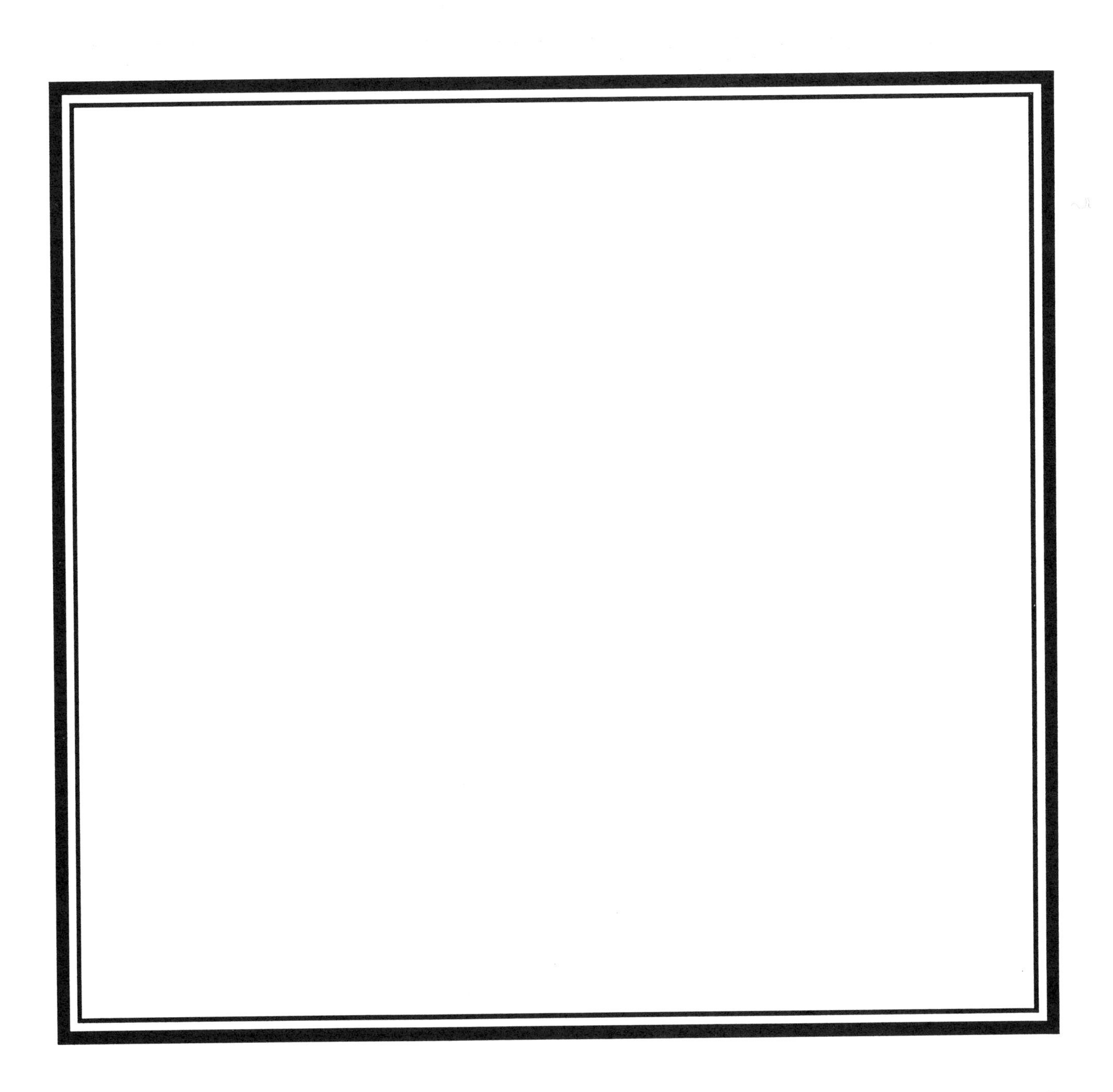

Activity Sheet 7

Anger at Work

Draw a picture of a way you can make your anger work for you, or a way you can use your anger to give you the power to make changes in yourself. Write if you don't want to draw.

Activity Sheet 8

Helpful Ways I Can Express Anger

RECOGNIZE

ACCEPT

RELAX

THINK

EVALUATE

CHOOSE

EXPRESS

Activity Sheet 9

Coping Strategies

Problem Situation 1

My mom and dad are having a terrible fight.
Dad is slapping Mom.

Coping Strategy

____

____

____

Problem Situation 2

My mom is asking me if she should get a divorce from my dad.

Coping Strategy

____

____

____

Problem Situation 3

I'm so worried that my mom is going to get hurt that I feel sick
and stay home from school.

Coping Strategy

____

____

____

Activity Sheet 10

My Personal Goals

For My Body:

____

____

____

____

For My Mind:

____

____

____

____

For My Feelings:

____

____

____

____

For My Choices:

____

____

____

____

Activity Sheet 11

People to talk to when I have a problem or feel sad or angry:

____

____

____

____

Safe places to go if my parents fight:

____

____

Important phone numbers:

Emergency:____________________

____

People to ask for help with schoolwork:

____

____

____

____

My Personal Yellow Pages

People to have fun with:

____

____

____

____

Basic Facts Worksheet 1

1. People in families have many kinds of FEELINGS, and all of these feelings are normal.

2. Some ways of showing feelings are HELPFUL; some ways of showing feelings are HARMFUL.

PRACTICE

1. People in families have many kinds of _______________ , and all of these feelings are normal.

2. Some ways of showing feelings are _________________ ; some ways of showing feelings are _________________ .

Basic Facts Worksheet 2

3. Some people choose to use VIOLENT ways to express their anger. They may yell, blame, throw, break, push, shove, kick, slap, hit, punch, or kill.

4. It is NEVER okay to use violent ways to express ANGER.

5. People can choose to learn NONVIOLENT and HELPFUL ways to express their anger.

PRACTICE

3. Some people choose to use ____________________ ways to express their anger. They may yell, blame, throw, break, push, shove, kick, slap, hit, punch, or kill.

4. It is _______________ okay to use violent ways to express

    _____________________.

5. People can choose to learn ___________________________

    and ____________________ ways to express their anger.

Basic Facts Worksheet 3

6. Parents usually LOVE their children, even when parents are choosing to use violent ways to express their anger.

7. Children usually LOVE their parents, although they may feel HATE for the parents if the parents are using violent ways to express their anger.

PRACTICE

6. Parents usually ____________ their children, even when parents are choosing to use violent ways to express their anger.

7. Children usually ____________ their parents, although they may feel ____________ for the parents if the parents are using violent ways to express their anger.

Basic Facts Worksheet 4

8. The three Cs are:
   1. Children don't CAUSE their parents to use violence to express their anger.
   2. Children can't CONTROL how their parents express anger.
   3. Children can't CHANGE their parents use of violence to express anger.

9. The four steps children can take are:
   1. Find a SAFE place for themselves.
   2. Ask a grown-up for HELP if the parents are out of control with their violence.
   3. Learn to RECOGNIZE, ACCEPT, and SHARE their feelings.
   4. Choose to learn NONVIOLENT ways to express their own feelings.

PRACTICE

8. The three Cs are:

   1. Children don't __________________________ their parents to use violence to express their anger.
   2. Children can't __________________________ how their parents express anger.
   3. Children can't __________________________ their parents' use of violence to express anger.

9. The four steps children can take are:

   1. Find a ______________________ place for themselves.
   2. Ask a grown-up for ________________ if the parents are out of control with their violence.
   3. Learn to ______________________________ , ________________________ , and ________________ their feelings.
   4. Choose to learn ________________________________ ways to express their own feelings.

Basic Facts Worksheet 5

10. Feelings aren't good or bad, or right or wrong; they just ARE.

11. Instead of swallowing feelings, it's better to RECOGNIZE them, ACCEPT them, and SHARE them with someone you trust.

PRACTICE

10. Feelings aren't good or bad, or right or wrong; they just ________________.

11. Instead of swallowing feelings, it's better to ________________________ them, __________________ them, and ______________ them with someone you trust.

Basic Facts Worksheet 6

12. When children are angry about a problem they can change, they should <u>USE</u> their anger to give them the power to make changes in themselves.

13. When children are angry about a problem they can't change, they should:

    1. <u>ACCEPT</u> what they can't change.
    2. <u>EXPRESS</u> their anger so they can let it <u>GO</u>.
    3. Do something <u>GOOD</u> for themselves.

PRACTICE

12. When children are angry about a problem they can change, they should ____________ their anger to give them the power to make changes in themselves.

13. When children are angry about a problem they cannot change, they should:

    1. ______________________ what they cannot change.
    2. _______________ their anger so they can let it _____.
    3. Do something ____________________ for themselves.

Basic Facts Worksheet 7

14. Anger management is a way to COPE with anger.

15. The anger management steps are:
    1. RECOGNIZE that you're angry.
    2. ACCEPT your anger.
    3. Practice some RELAXATION.
    4. THINK about ways to express the anger.
    5. EVALUATE the consequences.
    6. CHOOSE the best way.
    7. EXPRESS the anger in a helpful way.

PRACTICE

14. Anger management is a way to _______________ with anger.

15. The anger management steps are:

    1. ______________________________ that you're angry.
    2. ______________________________ your anger.
    3. Practice ______________________________.
    4. _________________ about ways to express the anger.
    5. ______________________________ the consequences.
    6. _________________________ the best way.
    7. ______________________ the anger in a helpful way.

Basic Facts Worksheet 8

16. Children can't FIX their parents' problems.

17. Children can take GOOD CARE of themselves.

PRACTICE

16. Children can't ____________ their parents' problems.

17. Children can take ______________________________ of themselves.

Basic Facts Worksheet 9

18. Children need to take care of their BODIES, their FEELINGS, their MINDS, and their CHOICES.

PRACTICE

18. Children need to take care of their ____________________, their ________________________, their ________________, and their ___________________________.

Basic Facts Worksheet 1

1. People in families have many kinds of FEELINGS, and all of these feelings are normal.

2. Some ways of showing feelings are HELPFUL; some ways of showing feelings are HARMFUL.

PRACTICE

1. People in families have many kinds of FEELINGS, and all of these feelings are normal.

2. Some ways of showing feelings are HELPFUL; some ways of showing feelings are HARMFUL.

Basic Facts Worksheet 2

3. Some people choose to use VIOLENT ways to express their anger. They may yell, blame, throw, break, push, shove, kick, slap, hit, punch, or kill.

4. It is NEVER okay to use violent ways to express ANGER.

5. People can choose to learn NONVIOLENT and HELPFUL ways to express their anger.

PRACTICE

3. Some people choose to use VIOLENT ways to express their anger. They may yell, blame, throw, break, push, shove, kick, slap, hit, punch, or kill.

4. It is NEVER okay to use violent ways to express ANGER.

5. People can choose to learn NONVIOLENT and HELPFUL ways to express their anger.

Basic Facts Worksheet 3

6. Parents usually LOVE their children, even when parents are choosing to use violent ways to express their anger.

7. Children usually LOVE their parents, although they may feel HATE for the parents if the parents are using violent ways to express their anger.

PRACTICE

6. Parents usually LOVE their children, even when parents are choosing to use violent ways to express their anger.

7. Children usually LOVE their parents, although they may feel HATE for the parents if the parents are using violent ways to express their anger.

Basic Facts Worksheet 4

8. The three Cs are:
   1. Children don't CAUSE their parents to use violence to express their anger.
   2. Children can't CONTROL how their parents express anger.
   3. Children can't CHANGE their parents use of violence to express anger.

9. The four steps children can take are:
   1. Find a SAFE place for themselves.
   2. Ask a grown-up for HELP if the parents are out of control with their violence.
   3. Learn to RECOGNIZE, ACCEPT, and SHARE their feelings.
   4. Choose to learn NONVIOLENT ways to express their own feelings.

PRACTICE

8. The three Cs are:
    1. Children don't CAUSE their parents to use violence to express their anger.
    2. Children can't CONTROL how their parents express anger.
    3. Children can't CHANGE their parents use of violence to express anger.

9. The four steps children can take are:
    1. Find a SAFE place for themselves.
    2. Ask a grown-up for HELP if the parents are out of control with their violence.
    3. Learn to RECOGNIZE, ACCEPT, and SHARE their feelings.
    4. Choose to learn NONVIOLENT ways to express their own feelings.

Basic Facts Worksheet 5

10. Feelings aren't good or bad, or right or wrong; they just ARE.

11. Instead of swallowing feelings, it's better to RECOGNIZE them, ACCEPT them, and SHARE them with someone you trust.

PRACTICE

10. Feelings aren't good or bad, or right or wrong; they just ARE.

11. Instead of swallowing feelings, it's better to RECOGNIZE them, ACCEPT them, and SHARE them with someone you trust.

Basic Facts Worksheet 6

12. When children are angry about a problem they can change, they should USE their anger to give them the power to make changes in themselves.

13. When children are angry about a problem they can't change, they should:

    1. ACCEPT what they can't change.
    2. EXPRESS their anger so they can let it GO.
    3. Do something GOOD for themselves.

PRACTICE

12. When children are angry about a problem they can change, they should USE their anger to give them the power to make changes in themselves.

13. When children are angry about a problem they can't change, they should:

    1. ACCEPT what they can't change.
    2. EXPRESS their anger so they can let it GO.
    3. Do something GOOD for themselves.

Basic Facts Worksheet 7

14. Anger management is a way to COPE with anger.

15. The anger management steps are:

    1. RECOGNIZE that you're angry.
    2. ACCEPT your anger.
    3. Practice some RELAXATION.
    4. THINK about ways to express the anger.
    5. EVALUATE the consequences.
    6. CHOOSE the best way.
    7. EXPRESS the anger in a helpful way.

PRACTICE

14. Anger management is a way to COPE with anger.

15. The anger management steps are:

    1. RECOGNIZE that you're angry.
    2. ACCEPT your anger.
    3. Practice some RELAXATION.
    4. THINK about ways to express the anger.
    5. EVALUATE the consequences.
    6. CHOOSE the best way.
    7. EXPRESS the anger in a helpful way.

Basic Facts Worksheet 8

16. Children can't FIX their parents' problems.

17. Children can take GOOD CARE of themselves.

PRACTICE

16. Children can't FIX their parents' problems.

17. Children can take GOOD CARE of themselves.

Basic Facts Worksheet 9

18. Children need to take care of their BODIES, their FEELINGS, their MINDS, and their CHOICES.

PRACTICE

18. Children need to take care of their BODIES, their FEELINGS, their MINDS, and their CHOICES.

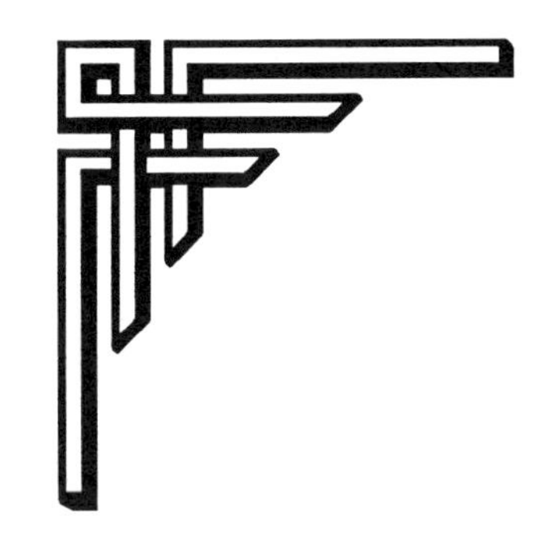

**People
in families
have many
kinds of
<u>FEELINGS,</u>
and all of
these feelings
are normal.**

2

Some ways of showing feelings are HELPFUL; some ways of showing feelings are HARMFUL.

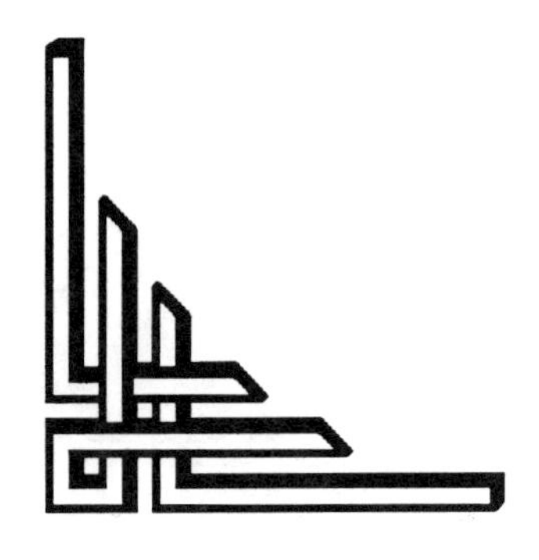
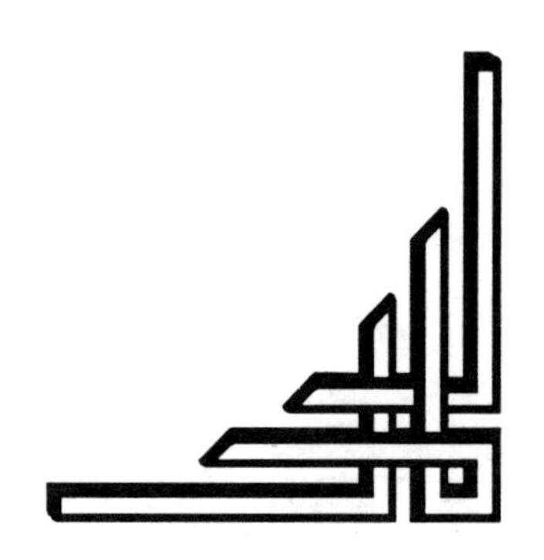

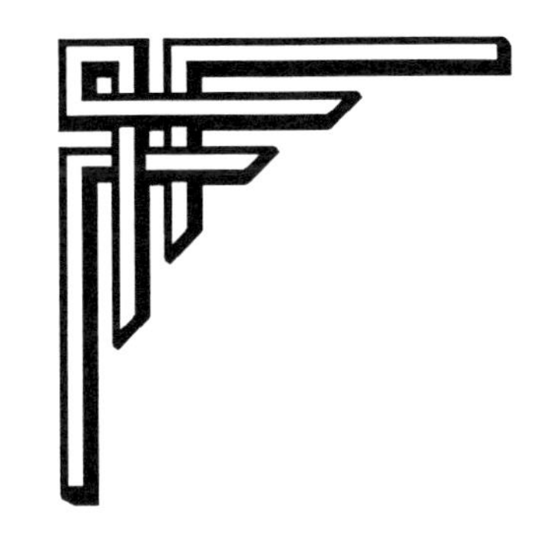

3

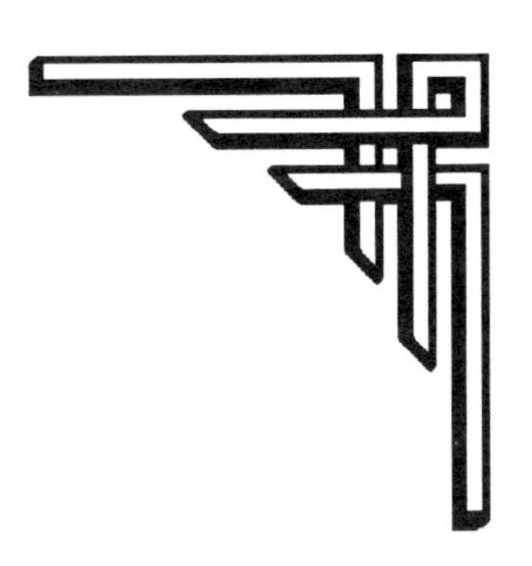

Some people
choose to use
VIOLENT ways
to express their anger.

They may yell,
blame, throw, break,
push, shove, kick,
slap, hit, punch, or kill.

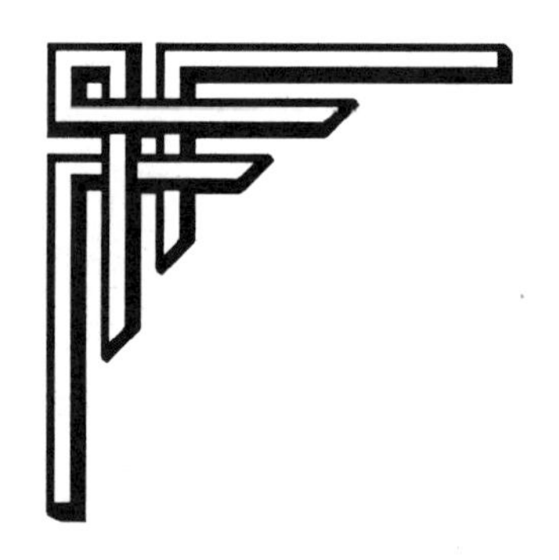

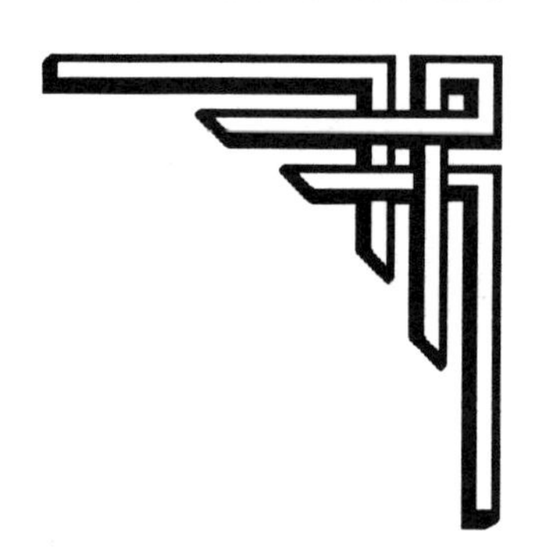

4

It is
<u>NEVER</u>
okay
to use
violent ways
to express
<u>ANGER</u>.

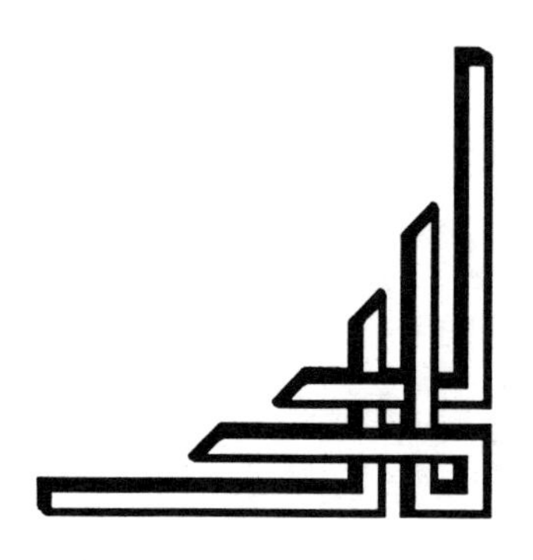

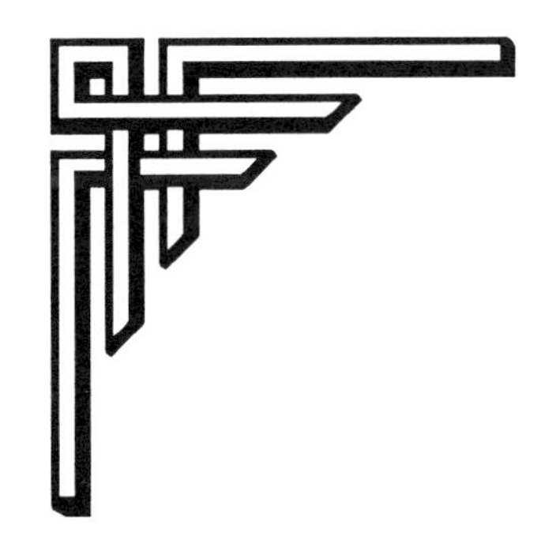

5

People can choose to learn NONVIOLENT and HELPFUL ways to express their anger.

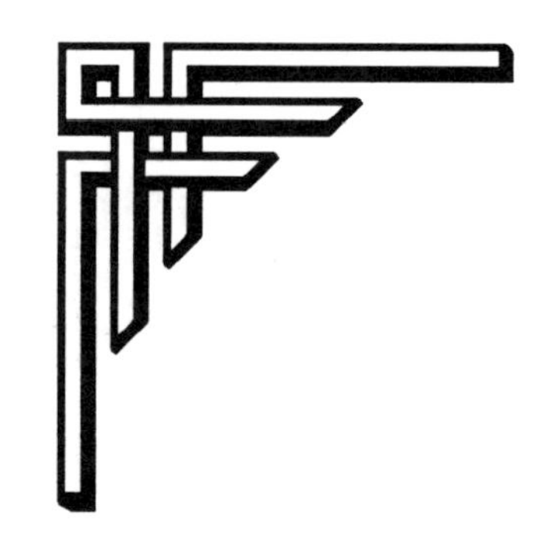

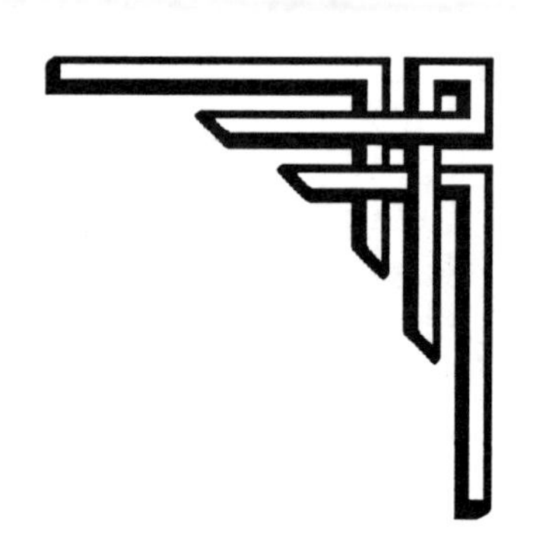

Parents usually
LOVE their children,
even when parents
are choosing to use
violent ways
to express
their anger.

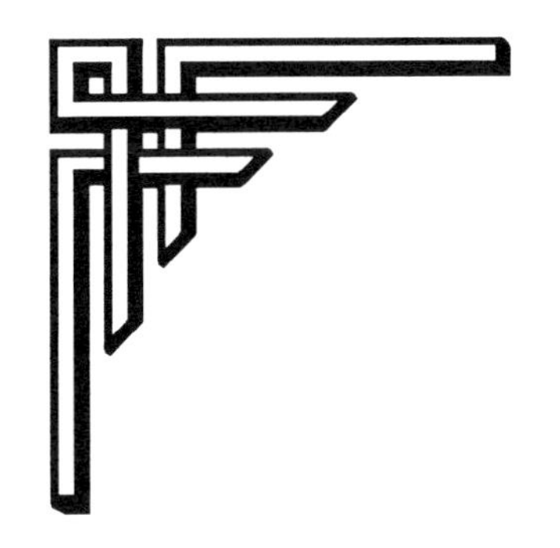

7

Children usually <u>LOVE</u> their parents, although they may feel <u>HATE</u> for the parents if the parents are using violent ways to express their anger.

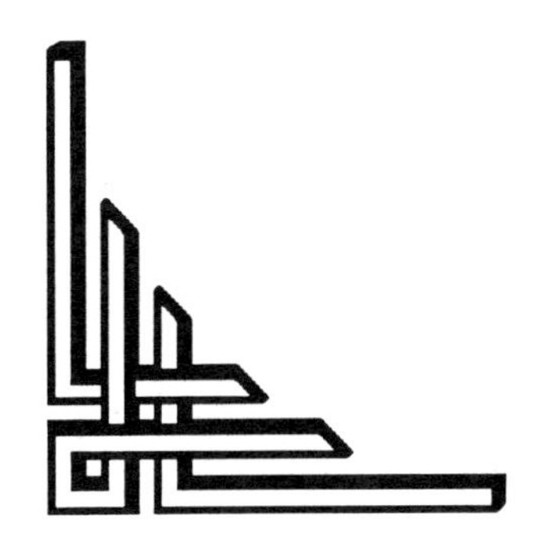

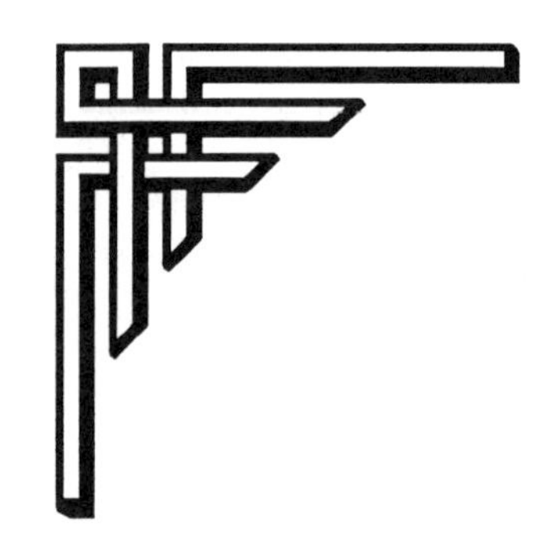

8

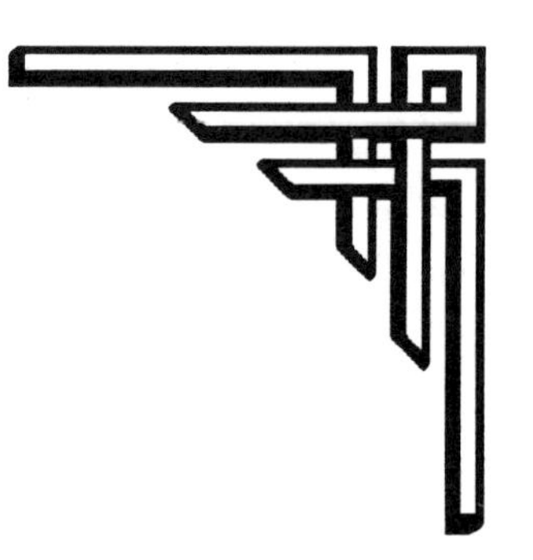

The three Cs are:

Children don't CAUSE their parents to use violence to express their anger.

Children can't CONTROL how their parents express anger.

Children can't CHANGE their parents' use of violence to express anger.

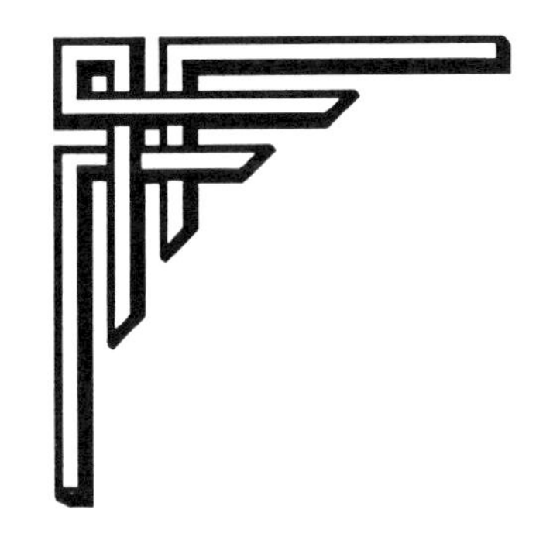

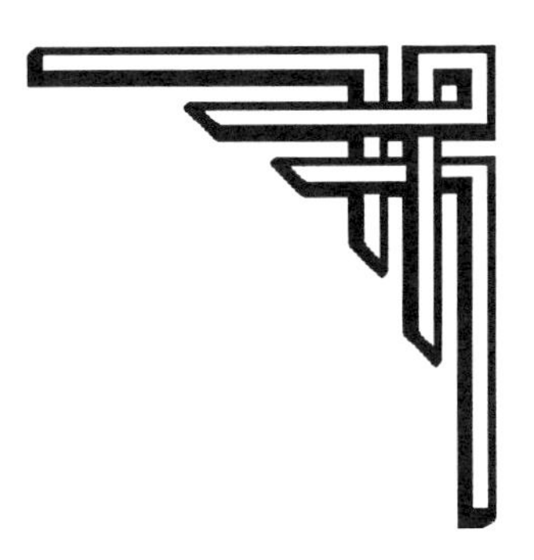

The four steps children can take are:

Find a SAFE place for themselves.

Ask a grown-up for HELP if the parents are out of control with their violence.

Learn to RECOGNIZE, ACCEPT, and SHARE their feelings.

Choose to learn NONVIOLENT ways to express their own feelings.

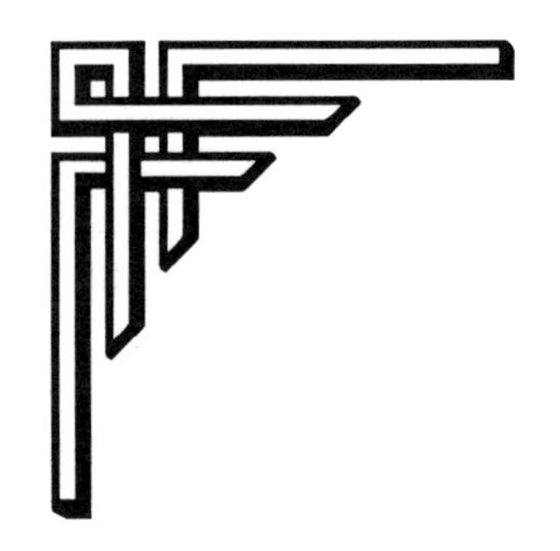

10

Feelings
aren't
good or bad,
right or wrong;
they just
ARE.

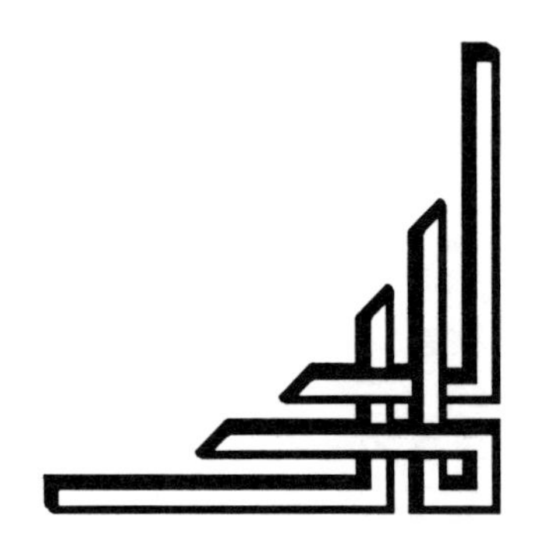

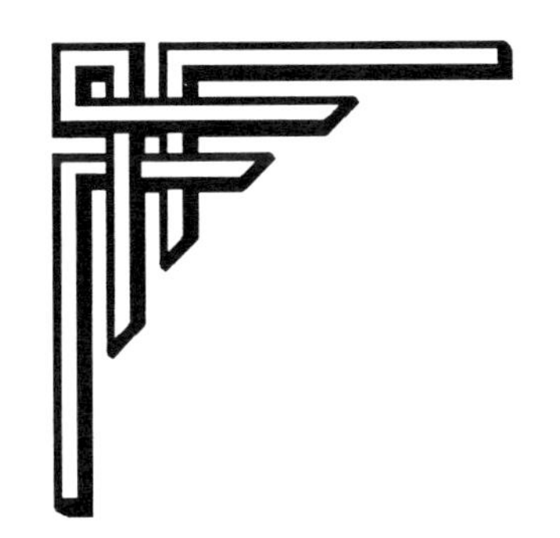

11

Instead of
swallowing feelings,
it's better to
RECOGNIZE them,
ACCEPT them,
and SHARE them
with someone
you trust.

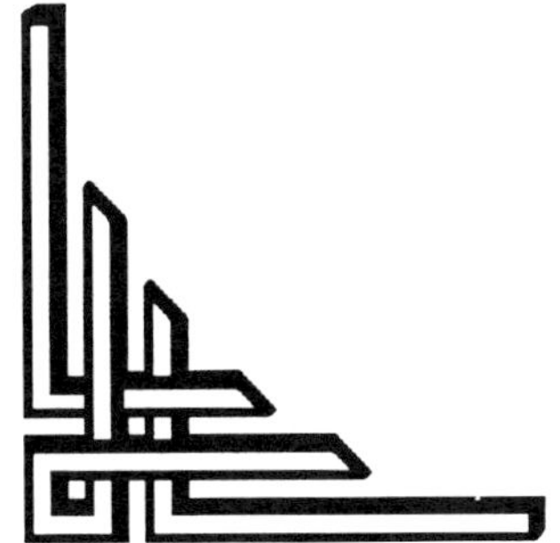

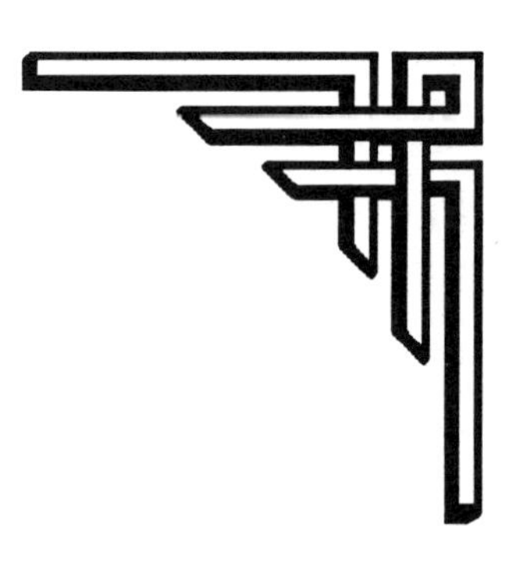

12

When children
are angry
about a problem
they can change,
they should
USE their anger
to give them the power
to make changes in
themselves.

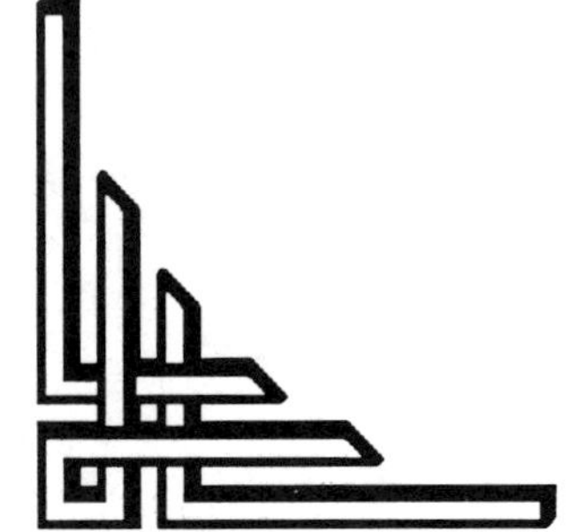

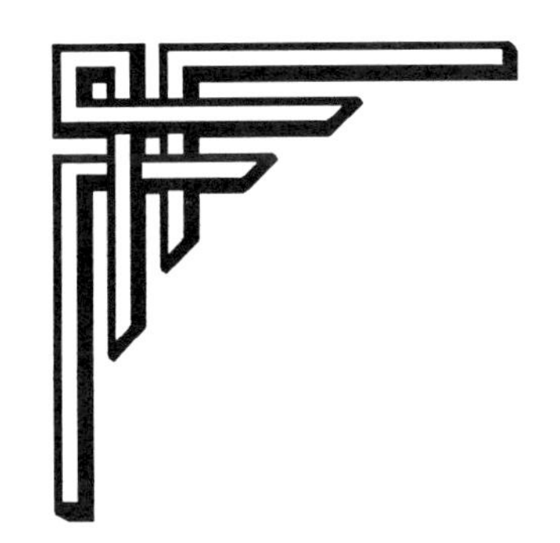

13

When children are angry about a problem they can't change, they should:

ACCEPT what they can't change.

EXPRESS their anger so they can let it GO.

Do something GOOD for themselves.

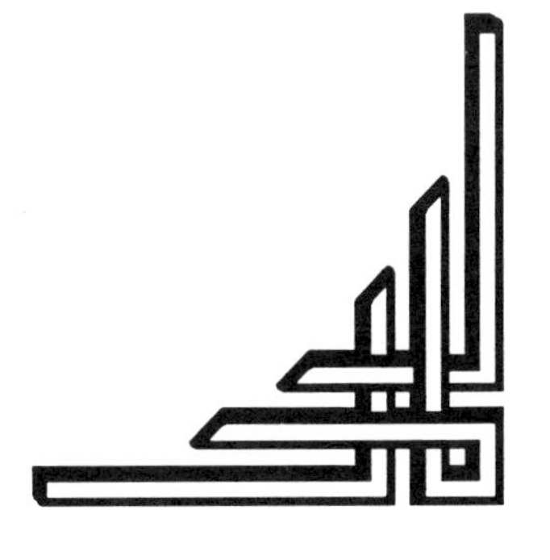

14

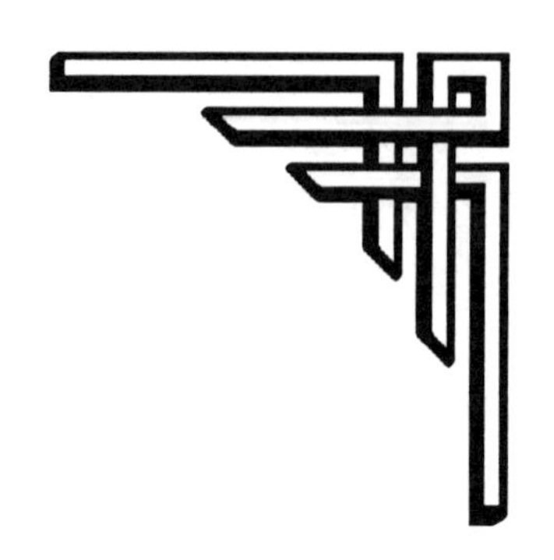

Anger management is a way to <u>COPE</u> with anger.

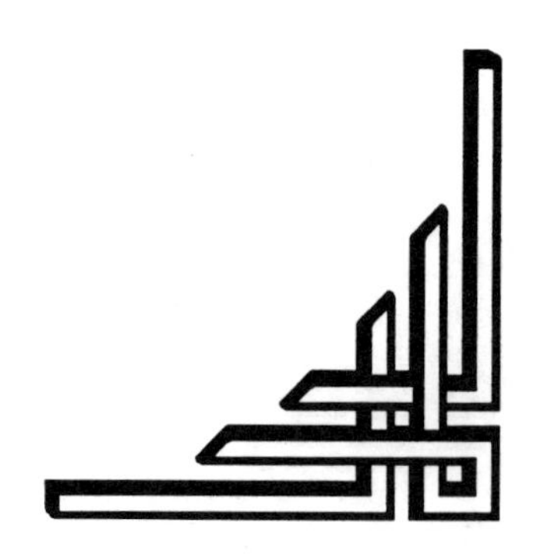

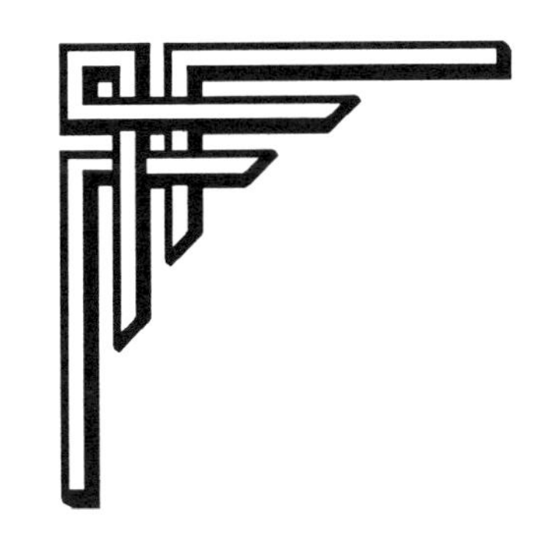

15

The anger management steps are:

RECOGNIZE that you're angry.

ACCEPT your anger.

Practice some RELAXATION.

THINK about ways to express the anger.

EVALUATE the consequences.

CHOOSE the best way.

EXPRESS the anger in a helpful way.

16

Children can't <u>FIX</u> their parents' problems.

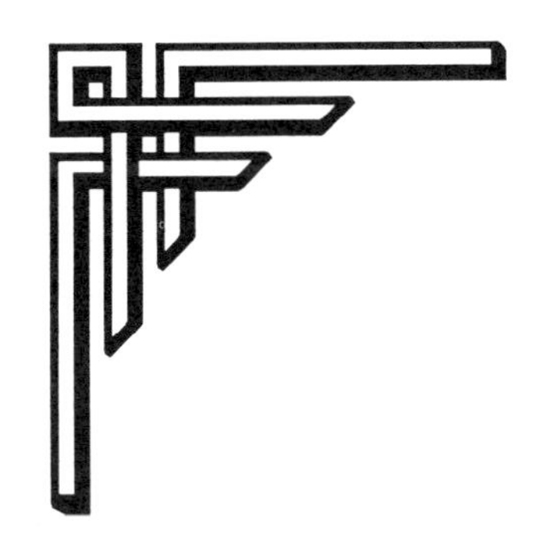

17

Children can take GOOD CARE of themselves.

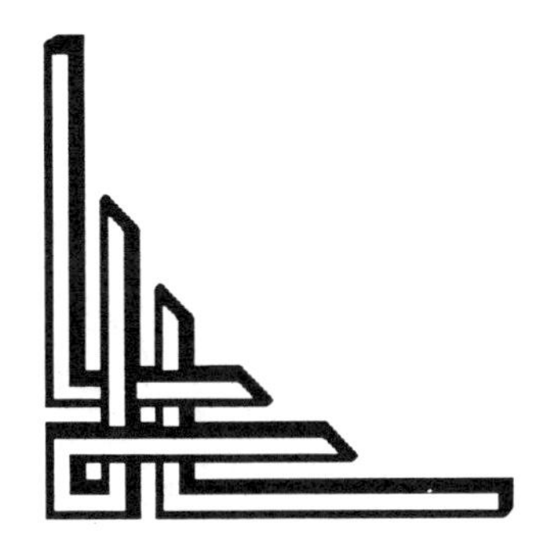

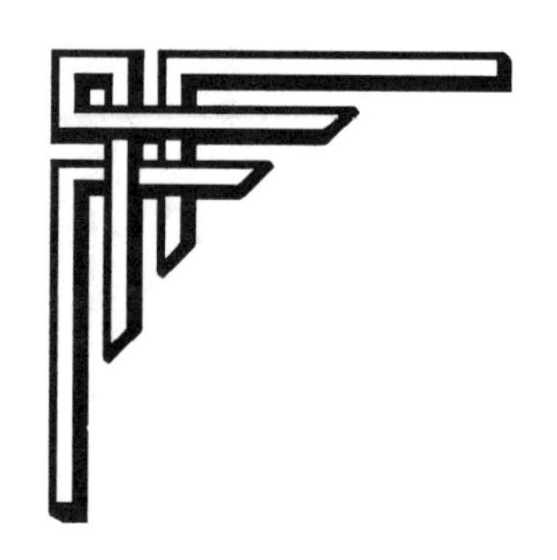
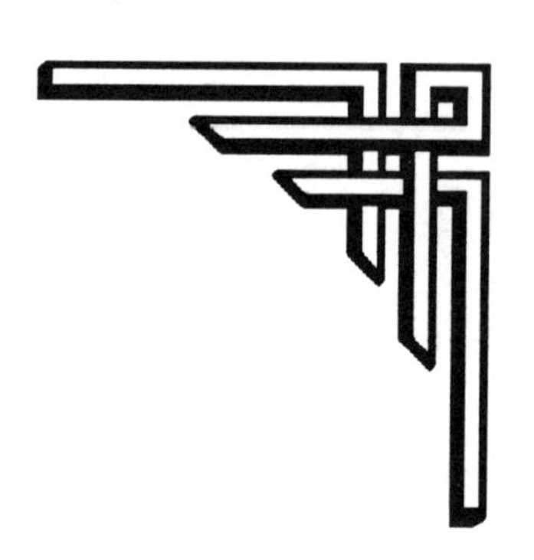

18

**Children need
to take care of
their BODIES,
their FEELINGS,
their MINDS,
and
their CHOICES.**

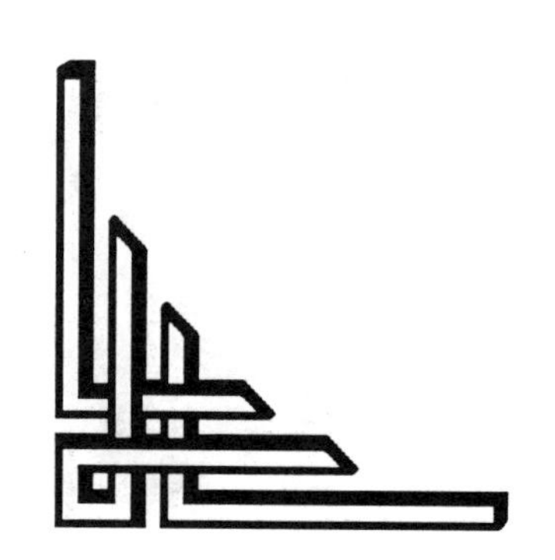
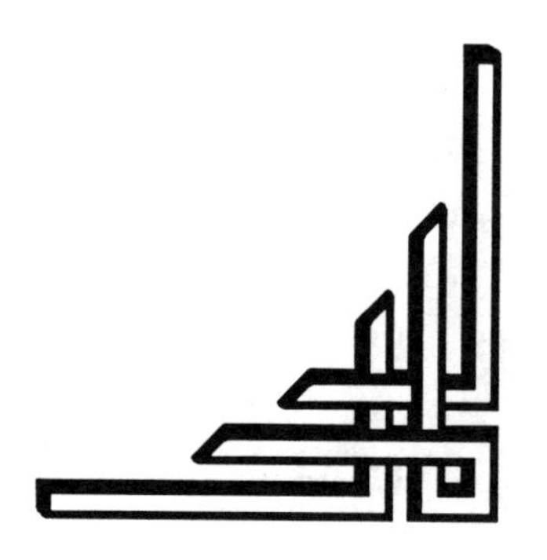

A Certificate of Participation
is awarded to

____

who has participated in a
Della the Dinosaur Group

Congratulations!

_______________ Leader's Name
_______________ Date
_______________ School

All the Basic Facts

1. People in families have many kinds of FEELINGS, and all of these feelings are normal.
2. Some ways of showing feelings are HELPFUL; some ways of showing feelings are HARMFUL.
3. Some people choose to use VIOLENT ways to express their anger. They may yell, blame, throw, break, push, shove, kick, slap, hit, punch, or kill.
4. It is NEVER okay to use violent ways to express ANGER.
5. People can choose to learn NONVIOLENT and HELPFUL ways to express their anger.
6. Parents usually LOVE their children, even when parents are choosing to use violent ways to express their anger.
7. Children usually LOVE their parents, although they may feel HATE for the parents if the parents are using violent ways to express their anger.
8. The three Cs are:
   1. Children don't CAUSE their parents to use violence to express their anger.
   2. Children can't CONTROL how their parents express anger.
   3. Children can't CHANGE their parents' use of violence to express anger.
9. The four steps children can take are:
   1. Find a SAFE place for themselves.
   2. Ask a grown-up for HELP if the parents are out of control with their violence.
   3. Learn to RECOGNIZE, ACCEPT, and SHARE their feelings.
   4. Choose to learn NONVIOLENT ways to express their own feelings.
10. Feelings aren't good or bad, right or wrong; they just ARE.
11. Instead of swallowing feelings, it's better to RECOGNIZE them, ACCEPT them, and SHARE them with someone you trust.
12. When children are angry about a problem they can change, they should USE their anger to give them the power to make changes in themselves.
13. When children are angry about a problem they can't change, they should:
    1. ACCEPT what they can't change.
    2. EXPRESS their anger so they can let it GO.
    3. Do something GOOD for themselves.
14. Anger management is a way to COPE with anger.
15. The anger management steps are:
    1. RECOGNIZE that you're angry.
    2. ACCEPT your anger.
    3. Practice some RELAXATION.
    4. THINK about ways to express the anger.
    5. EVALUATE the consequences.
    6. CHOOSE the best way.
    7. EXPRESS the anger in a helpful way.
16. Children can't FIX their parents' problems.
17. Children can take GOOD CARE of themselves.
18. Children need to take care of their BODIES, their FEELINGS, their MINDS, and their CHOICES.

Audience Evaluation Form

1. The most interesting thing I learned from this presentation was____
____

2. How much impact do you think this presentation will have on your use of harmful ways to express feelings? (circle one)

None Some Much

In what way?

____
____

If you're interested in being in a group like Della the Dinosaur because you'd like to discuss problems and issues that arise when you or someone you live with uses harmful ways to express anger, please sign here. We will keep your name confidential, but will contact you about your concern soon.

Name: ____

Teacher's name or home room number: ________________________

Grade and school you will attend next year: ________________________

Group Evaluation Form

1. What did you like best about this group?

   ____

   ____

2. What did you like least about this group?

   ____

   ____

3. What do you think should be done differently?

   ____

   ____

4. What would have made the group more helpful to you?

   ____

   ____

5. What do you think is the most important thing you learned from this group?

   ____

   ____

6. What is one good thing that's happened to you because you were in this group?

   ____

   ____

7. As a result of being in this group, how have you changed?

   ____

   ____

Process and Progress Form

Leader's Name:________________________ Session #:____ Date:_________

Children (group members) present:

____

____

Processing the Session

1. What were the objectives of this session?

   ____

2. How were they met?

   ____

3. What concepts must the leader understand to facilitate this session effectively?

   ____

4. What happened during the session?

   Highs:

   ____

   Lows:

   ____

5. What did you see as your strengths as you facilitated this session?

   ____

6. What changes would you make for the next time?

   ____

Noting Progress:

____

____

Progress Notes

Group: ____

Members of Group: ______________________________________

____

Session 1: Date: ______________

Notes: ____

____

____

Session 2: Date: ______________

Notes: ____

____

____

Session 3: Date: ______________

Notes: ____

____

____

Session 4: Date: ______________

Notes: ____

____

____

Session 5: Date: ______________

Notes: ____

____

____

Session 6: Date: ____________________

Notes: ____

____

____

Session 7: Date: ____________________

Notes: ____

____

____

Session 8: Date: ____________________

Notes: ____

____

____

Session 9: Date: ____________________

Notes: ____

____

____

Session 10: Date: ____________________

Notes: ____

____

____

Session 11: Date: ____________________

Notes: ____

____

____

Self-Referral Group Survey Form

Dear Student,

The Pupil Services Staff of (*Name of School*) is very pleased to offer five fun and exciting groups that you can join. These groups will meet once a week during the school day for eleven weeks. Group meetings last about 45 minutes.

Look at the list of groups below. Put an "X" by the group or groups you would like to join. If you think you'd like to be in more than one group, please number them in priority.

______ Peter the Puppy Group (If you're worried about someone who's using alcohol or other drugs.)

______ Thomas Barker Group (If you belong to a family that's separated or divorced, has only one parent, or has a stepparent.)

______ Della the Dinosaur Group (If you or someone close to you uses harmful ways to show anger.)

______ Daniel the Dinosaur Group (If you are often being bullied by others.)

______ Trevor and Tiffany Group (If you treat others in a mean way.)

Name ____

Teacher ____

We'll meet with you soon to talk about the group(s) you chose.

Thank you,

(Signatures of program coordinator, group leader, guidance counselor, and/or school social worker)

Parental Consent Letter

Dear Parent,

As part of our Substance Abuse Prevention Program, the Pupil Services Staff of *(Name of School)* will be offering children a chance to take part in a special group process called *Della the Dinosaur Talks About Violence and Anger Management.*

This group will teach group members about: (1) identifying feelings; (2) helpful and harmful ways of expressing feelings; (3) the effects of violence on children; (4) anger management; (5) coping strategies; (6) setting personal goals; and (7) developing a support system.

The group will be held during the regular school day. It will be led by *(Name of leader and necessary credentials).* As a teaching technique, we like to have the children make a presentation about what they've learned.

Unless we hear otherwise from you, we'll assume we have your permission for your child to participate in the group. Please know that we treat all information with the strictest confidentiality and the highest respect. If you have any questions or concerns about the group, please call me at *(phone number).*

We think that the group will be an exciting and positive experience for your child, and we're happy to be able to offer it.

Thank you for your cooperation and participation.

Sincerely,

(Signature of school social worker.)

Screening Interview Outline

Use this outline to screen prospective group members.

Name:______________________________ Date:______________________________

Age: ______________________________ Date of Birth:______________________

Grade: _____________________________ Teacher's Name:____________________

Feelings about school:____

____

Grades in school:____

School adjustment: ____

____

Home Address: ____

Phone: ____

Who lives in the house with the child?_____________________________________

____

If parents divorced, where does each live?_________________________________

____

Visitation? ____

What does the child do after school?_______________________________________

____

Typical daily schedule:____

____

Hobbies, clubs, sports: ____

____

Strengths: ____

____

Weaknesses: ____

____

Stresses in life:____

____

References and Suggested Readings

Ackerman, R. 1983. *Children of alcoholics: A guidebookfor educators, therapists, and parents.* Holmes Beach, FL: Learning Publications, Inc.

Beattie, M. 1987. *Co-dependent no more.* San Francisco: Harper/Hazelden.

Black, C. 1981. *It will never happen to me.* Newport Beach, CA: ACT.

Cermak, T. 1985. *A primer on adult children of alcoholics.* Deerfield Beach, FL: Health Communications.

Davis, D. 1984. *Something is wrong at my house.* Seattle: Parenting Press, Inc.

Davis, D. 1986. *Working with children from violent homes.* Santa Cruz, CA: Network Publications, ETR Associates.

Everstine, D.L. 1986. *People in crises: Strategic therapeutic interventions.* New York: Bruner/Mazel.

Friel, J., and L. Friel. 1988. *Adult children: The secrets of dysfunctional families.* Deerfield Beach, FL: Health Communications, Inc.

Hunter, M. 1983. *Mastery teaching.* El Segundo, CA: TIP Publications.

Kalter, N. 1990. *Growing up with divorce.* New York: The Free Press.

Leite, E., and P. Espeland. 1987. *Different like me.* Minneapolis: Johnson Institute.

Lerner, H. 1985. *The dance of anger.* New York: Harper & Row.

Lystad, M. 1986. *Violence in the home—interdisciplinary perspective.* New York: Bruner/ Mazel Publishers.

McGinnis, E., and A. P. Goldstein. 1984. *Skill-streaming the elementary school child.* Champaign, IL: Research Press Company.

Oates, D. 1987. *Child abuse and neglect—what happens eventually?* New York: Bruner/ Mazel Publishers.

Piaget, J. 1928. *Judgment and reasoning in the child.* New York: Harcourt, Brace, Jovanovich.

Sanford, T. 1990. *Strong at the broken places.* New York: Random House.

Saunders, A., and B. Remsberg. 1984. *The stress proof child.* New York: Holt Rinehart and Winston.

Typpo, M., and J. Hastings. 1984. *An elephant in the living room.* Center City, MN: Hazelden.

Wahl, A., and B. Kaufman.1986. *Silent screams and hidden cries, an interpretation of art work by children from violent homes.* New York: Bruner/Mazel Publishers.

Wegscheider-Cruse, S. 1980. *Another chance: Hope and health for the alcoholic family.* Palo Alto, CA: Science and Behavior Books.

Weisinger, H. 1985. *Dr. Weisinger's anger work-out book.* Syracuse, NY: Evaluation Research Associates, Inc.

Other Resources

The following materials are available from the Johnson Institute. Call us at 800-231-5165 for ordering information, current prices, or a complete listing of Johnson Institute resources.

Video Programs

An Attitude Adjustment for Ramie. 15 minutes. Order #V429

Anger: Handle It Before It Handles You. 15 minutes. Order #V450

Broken Toy. 30 minutes. Order #V462

Choices & Consequences. 33 minutes. Order #V400

Conflict: Think About It, Talk About It, Try To Work It Out. 15 minutes. Order #V451

Dealing with Anger: A Violence Prevention Program for African-American Youth. 52 minutes (males), 68 minutes (females). Order #V433 (for males); Order #V456 (for females)

Double Bind. 15 minutes. Order #V430

Good Intentions, Bad Results. 30 minutes. Order #V440

It's Not Okay To Bully. 15 minutes. Order #5883JH

Peer Mediation: Conflict Resolution in Schools. 28 minutes. Order #V458Kit

Respect & Protect: A Solution To Stopping Violence in Schools and Communities. 28 minutes. Order #460

Tulip Doesn't Feel Safe. 12 minutes. Order #V438

Publications

Bosch, Carl W. *Bully on the Bus*. Order #P413

Boyd, Lizi. *Bailey the Big Bully*. Order #P422

Carlson, Nancy. *Loudmouth George and the Sixth-Grade Bully*. Order #P414

Crary, Elizabeth. *I Can't Wait*. Order #P431

______. *I'm Furious*. Order #P506

______. *I'm Mad*. Order #P509

______. *I Want It*. Order #P427

______. *My Name Is Not Dummy*. Order #P429

Cummings, Carol. *I'm Always in Trouble*. Order #P418

______. *Sticks and Stones*. Order #P420

______. *Tattlin' Madeline*. Order #P421

______. *Win, Win Day*. Order #P419

Davis, Diane. *Working with Children from Violent Homes: Ideas and Techniques*. Order #P244

DeMarco, John. *Peer Helping Skills Program for Training Peer Helpers and Peer Tutors*. Order #P320Kit

Estes, Eleanor. *The Hundred Dresses*. Order #P411

Fleming, Martin. *Conducting Support Groups for Students Affected by Chemical Dependence: A Guide for Educators and Other Professionals*. Order #P020

Freeman, Shelley MacKay. *From Peer Pressure to Peer Support: Alcohol and Other Drug Prevention through Group Process*. Order #P147-7-8 (for grades 7 and 8); Order #P147-9-10 (for grades 9 and 10); Order #P147-11-12 (for grades 11 and 12)

Garbarino, James, et al. *Children in Danger*. Order #P330

Goldstein, Arnold P., et al. *Aggression Replacement Training: A Comprehensive Intervention for Aggressive Youth*. Order #P329

Haven, Kendall. *Getting Along*. Order #P412

Johnsen, Karen. *The Trouble With Secrets*. Order #P425

Johnson Institute's No-Bullying Program for Grades K-Middle School. Order #546Kit

Julik, Edie. *Sailing Through the Storm to the Ocean of Peace*. Order #P437

Lawson, Ann. *Kids & Gangs: What Parents and Educators Need To Know*. Order #P322

Mills, Lauren. *The Rag Coat*. Order #P417

Moe, Jerry, and Peter Ways, M.D. *Conducting Support Groups for Elementary Chidren K-6.* Order #P123

Olofsdotter, Marie. *Frej the Fearless.* Order #P438

Perry, Kate, and Charlotte Firmin. *Being Bullied.* Order #P416

Peterson, Julie, and Rebecca Janke. *Peacemaker® Program*. Order #P447

Potter-Efron, Ron. *How To Control Your Anger (Before It Controls You): A Guide for Teenagers.* Order #P277

Remboldt, Carole. *Solving Violence Problems in Your School: Why A Systematic Approach Is Necessary*. Order #P336

______. *Violence in Schools: The Enabling Factor.* Order #P337

Remboldt, Carole, and Richard Zimman, Ph.D. *Respect & Protect: A Practical, Step-by-Step Violence Prevention and Intervention Program for Schools and Communities.* Order #P404

Sanders, Mark. *Preventing Gang Violence in Your School.* Order #P403

Saunders, Carol Silverman. *Safe at School: Awareness and Action for Parents of Kids in Grades K-12.* Order #P340

Schaefer, Dick. *Choices & Consequences: What To Do When a Teenager Uses Alcohol/Drugs.* Order #P096

Schmidt, Teresa. *Anger Management and Violence Prevention: A Group Activities Manual for Middle and High School Students.* Order #P278

______. *Changing Families: A Group Activities Manual for Middle and High School Students.* Order #P317

______. *Daniel the Dinosaur Learns To Stand Tall Against Bullies: A Group Activities Manual To Teach K-6 Children How To Handle Other Children's Aggressive Behavior.* Order #P559

______. *Trevor and Tiffany, The Tyrannosaurus Twins, Learn To Stop Bullying: A Group Activities Manual To Teach K-6 Children How To Replace Aggressive Behavior with Assertive Behavior*. Order #P558

Schott, Sue. *Everyone Can Be Your Friend*. Order #P435

Stine, Megan, and H. William Stine. *How I Survived 5th Grade*. Order #P415

Vernon, Ann. *Thinking, Feeling, Behaving.* (for grades 1-6) Order #P250

Villaume, Philip G., and R. Michael Foley. *Teachers at Risk: Crisis in the Classroom*. Order #P401

Wilmes, David. *Parenting for Prevention: How To Raise a Child To Say No to Alcohol/Drugs.* Order #P071

______. *Parenting for Prevention: A Parent Education Curriculum—Raising a Child To Say No to Alcohol and Other Drugs.* Order #P072TK

Resources for Help

Center for the Prevention of Sexual & Domestic Violence
1914 N. 34th Street, Suite 105
Seattle, WA 98103
206-634-1903

Center for Women Policy Studies
2000 P. Street, N.W., Suite 508
Washington, DC 20036
202-872-1770

COAF
Children of Alcoholics Foundation, Inc.
555 Madison Avenue, 4th Floor
New York, NY 10022
(212) 754-0656
800-359-COAF

Family Research Institute
University of New Hampshire
128 Horton Social Science Center
Durham, NH 03824
603-862-2761

Family Violence and Sexual Assault Institute
1310 Clinic Drive
Tyler, TX 75701
903-595-6600

Johnson Institute
7205 Ohms Lane
Minneapolis, MN 55439-2159
1-800-231-5165
(612) 831-1630

National Center on Child Abuse and Neglect
Clearinghouse on Child Abuse and Neglect Information
P.O. Box 1182
Washington, DC 20013-1182
703-385-7565 or 800-394-3366

NCADD
National Council on Alcoholism and Drug Dependence
12 West 21st Street
New York, NY 10010
(212) 206-6770

National Council on Child Abuse and Family Violence
1155 Connecticut Avenue, N.W., Suite 400
Washington, D.C. 20036
202-429-6695

National Criminal Justice Reference Service
1600 Research Boulevard
Rockville, MD 20850
800-851-3420

ORDER FORM

BILL TO:

Name ______________________

Address ______________________

____

City ______________ State ______ Zip ______

ATTENTION: ______________________

Daytime Phone: (   ) ______________________

PURCHASE ORDER NO. ______________________

❑ Individual Order ❑ Group or Organization Order

If Ordering for a Group or Organization:

Group Name ______________________

SHIP TO: (if different from BILL TO)

Name ______________________

Address ______________________

____

City ______________ State ______ Zip ______

ATTENTION: ______________________

Daytime Phone: (   ) ______________________

TAX EXEMPT NO. ______________________

Please send me a free copy(ies) of Johnson Institute's:

❑ ___ Publications and Films Catalog(s)
❑ ___ Training Calendar(s)
❑ *Observer*, a quarterly newsletter

PLEASE SEND ME:

QTY.	ORDER NO.	TITLE	PRICE EACH	TOTAL COST

For film/video titles, please specify: ❑ 1/2" VHS ❑ 3/4" U-Matic ❑ 1/2" Beta ❑ 16mm

SHIPPING AND HANDLING

Order Amount	U.S.	Outside U.S.
$0–25.00	$ 6.50	$8.00
$25.01–60.00	$ 8.50	$10.00
$60.01–130.00	$10.50	$13.50
$130.01–200.00	$13.25	$19.50
$200.01–300.00	$16.00	$24.00
$300.01–over	8%	14%

Please add $8.00 ($10.50 Canada) for any videotapes ordered.

OFFICE USE ONLY

Order No. ______________

Customer No. ______________

❑ Payment enclosed
❑ Bill me
❑ Bill my credit card:

❑ MasterCard
❑ VISA
❑ American Express
❑ Discover

Expiration Date: ______________

Signature on card: ______________

Total Order ______
(Orders under $75.00 must be prepaid)

6.5% Sales Tax ______
(Minnesota Residents Only)

Shipping and Handling ______
(See Chart)

TOTAL ______

Have you ordered from the Johnson Institute before? **Yes** ❑ **No** ❑
If yes, how? **Mail** ❑ **Phone** ❑

QVS, Inc.

JOHNSON INSTITUTE®

7205 Ohms Lane ❖ Minneapolis, Minnesota 55439-2159
(612) 831-1630 or toll-free: 1-800-231-5165

NOTES